LLEWELLYN'S
Little Book of
TAROT

Tyler Mielke

At a party in the early 1990s, someone put a tarot deck in Barbara's hands; she's held on tight ever since. She believes tarot provides just enough structure so that we don't get lost as we explore the mysteries, plumb our dark corners, and locate our guiding stars.

Barbara has published a number of books, including *Tarot for Beginners*, *Tarot Spreads*, *The Steampunk Tarot*, *Tarot in Wonderland*, and *Modern Guide to Energy Clearing*. She teaches tarot all over the world but mostly loves to be at home, writing, thinking, and playing with her cards. Barbara lives in beautiful northern California with her wife.

LLEWELLYN'S
Little Book of
TAROT

BARBARA MOORE

LLEWELLYN PUBLICATIONS
WOODBURY, MINNESOTA

FIRST EDITION
Fourth Printing, 2022

Book design by Rebecca Zins
Cover cartouche by Freepik
Cover design by Lisa Novak and Shira Atakpu
Llewellyn Publications is a registered trademark of Llewellyn Worldwide Ltd.

Library of Congress Cataloging-in-Publication Data

Names: Moore, Barbara, author.
Title: Llewellyn's little book of tarot / Barbara Moore.
Description: FIRST EDITION. | Woodbury : Llewellyn Worldwide, Ltd., 2019. |
  Series: Llewellyn's little books ; #8 | Includes bibliographical
  references.
Identifiers: LCCN 2018059302 (print) | LCCN 2019001674 (ebook) | ISBN
  9780738760032 (ebook) | ISBN 9780738759975 (alk. paper)
Subjects: LCSH: Tarot.
Classification: LCC BF1879.T2 (ebook) | LCC BF1879.T2 M6523 2019 (print) |
  DDC 133.3/2424—dc23
LC record available at https://lccn.loc.gov/2018059302

Llewellyn Worldwide Ltd. does not participate in, endorse, or have any authority or responsibility concerning private business transactions between our authors and the public.

All mail addressed to the author is forwarded, but the publisher cannot, unless specifically instructed by the author, give out an address or phone number.

Any internet references contained in this work are current at publication time, but the publisher cannot guarantee that a specific location will continue to be maintained. Please refer to the publisher's website for links to authors' websites and other sources.

Llewellyn Publications
A Division of Llewellyn Worldwide Ltd.
2143 Wooddale Drive
Woodbury, MN 55125-2989
www.llewellyn.com

Printed in China

To Benjamin and Lily,
the best proof that good things
come in little packages,
with much love
from Auntie Barbara

Strength • Tarot of the Magical Forest

Contents

Introduction   1

1: History...11

2: Structure and Symbolism 17

3: The Major Arcana 23

4: The Minor Arcana...........................71

5: Readings 193

6: Activities 209

Conclusion   223

Further Reading   225

Featured Decks   231

Exercises

1: Bibliomancy 4

2: Tarot Birth Cards.. 24

3: What's the Story? 198

4: Card of the Day 212

5: Tarot Journaling...215

6: Create an Affirmation 218

7: Meditation...220

8: Make Art... 222

Tarot Tips

1: Card Pairs, Part 1...................................... 35

2: Choices 39

3: Create a Spread 43

4: Hermit Time 45

5: Yearly Reading... 65

6: The Fool's Journey 69

7: Card Pairs, Part 2.......................................75

8: Easy vs. Hard Choices................................ 77

9: Telling a Story 79

10: Prioritizing..87

11: Resetting Your Deck 89

12: Personal Anecdotes 91

13: Be a Leader.............................101

14: Exalting Aces..........................105

15: Relationships 107

16: Negative Meanings.....................115

17: Elemental Advice 117

18: What Your Heart Wants 119

19: Dedicated Decks.......................123

20: Pages as Messages 125

21: Court Cards Ranks and Suits............131

22: When Cards Are Confusing..............141

23: Description and Prescription 143

24: Unequal Relationships..................145

25: Reading for Yourself...................147

26: Reversals, Part 1.......................149

27: Trimming a Deck.......................153

28: Correspondences 155

29: When to Save and When to Spend 171

30: Influencing Decision-Makers 175

31: Tarot Journey Check-In....................177

32: Positive Cards, Negative Positions............179

33: Court Card Connections............................189

34: Storing Tarot Decks......................191

35: Tiny Decks 194

36: Fanning Powder 196

37: Reversals, Part 2 197

38: What Wasn't Asked 202

39: Copying the Cards 210

40: Negative Cards 213

41: Selecting Your Tarot Journal......................216

Symbolism

1: The Fool's Dog.................................27

2: The High Priestess 31

3: The Keys..37

4: Wheel of Fortune..............................47

5: Justice and Consequences 49

6: Death.. 53

7: The Tower 59

8: The Moon.. 63

9: Numbers 81

10: Salamanders................................... 83

11: A Heavy Load................................... 93

12: Animal Companions 95

13: Knight of Wands 97

14: Sunflowers and Cats 99

15: Grief 113

16: Things That Are Held 129

17: The Ace of Swords..............................135

18: Truce 137

19: The Nine of Swords 151

20: Birds..159

21: The King of Swords and Chess.................161

22: Pentacles 165

23: The Two of Pentacles...........................167

24: How to Make Something Great 169

25: The Nine of Pentacles..........................181

26: The Ten of Pentacles 183

27: The Page of Pentacles 185

Journal Prompts

1: Beginning a Project...............................29

2: Mother Issues 33

3: Growing Up 41

4: Sacrifice 51

5: A Temperate Life................................... 55

6: Who Are Your Devils? 57

7: Forgiveness 61

8: Rebirth 67

9: Scarcity Mentality.. 85

10: Best Friends..109

11: Boredom...111

12: You as the Nine of Cups 121

13: How You Serve.. 127

14: When Truth Hurts 139

15: Planning and Strategy..................................157

16: Community 173

17: Knights Good and Bad 187

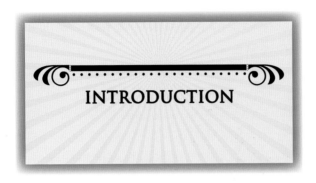

INTRODUCTION

• • •

Years ago, I attended a FaerieCon to introduce the Mystic Faerie Tarot and was on a panel about divination. Someone in the audience asked those of us on the panel about childhood experiences with divination. The other two panelists had charming stories about wandering the English countryside and getting messages from the plants and animals around them. My childhood was not so picturesque, taking place as it did in a newly constructed suburb of Detroit. However, no matter where humans live, we still turn to our environment for signs, messages, and inspiration. We read what surrounds us.

Divination for me as a child looked like this:

- Sit by the window facing the road.

- Make a wish.

- Set an intention like "if the third car that drives past is red, my wish will come true."

- Wait for three cars to drive by.

Maybe it was the suburban childhood, maybe it was just my nature, but I was always fascinated with systems and patterns and less inclined to commune with a flower. In fact, I was decidedly left-brained. Tarot bridged the gap between logic and intuition, thereby broadening my world. As if directed by some unseen forces, tarot entered my life at just the right moment.

As I was thoroughly enjoying my liberal arts college experience, I didn't realize that my mind was primed for the introduction of tarot, which happened at a party. Even though at the time I knew nothing about tarot except that people used the cards to tell fortunes, something told me that these seventy-eight pieces of paper were something special. It was true: the cards combined so many things that I loved, including history, art, mythology, and psychology. The moment was memorable, but of course I didn't realize how important the cards would become to me. I didn't know they would connect so many interests and also would connect my mind and my heart. I didn't know they would become my sacred text, a text that was flexible and generative enough to hold my ever-evolving understanding of spirituality and the world.

Back then, there weren't many books available, and the internet wasn't really a thing. Two of the first books I read were Mary K. Greer's *Tarot for Your Self* and Rachel Pollack's *78 Degrees of Wisdom*. These books, along with Sallie Nichols's *Jung and Tarot*, formed my tarot foundation. They showed me that tarot could be so much more than a way to divine the future.

It isn't necessary to make tarot a central focus of your life in order to enjoy or benefit from the cards. You don't need to study or memorize anything any more than you have to understand a natal chart, houses, decans, etc., to read your horoscope. It is possible to find comfort, advice, or inspiration from a single tarot card in the same way that you can benefit from the wisdom of a single quote. You don't need to read the collected works of Ram Dass, Rumi, or Einstein in order to be blessed by a short excerpt from their work. Don't let overwhelm keep you from enjoying the insights of the cards.

Throughout this book you will find fun and easy ways to use the cards. You will also get a peek into the vast world of tarot. There are hundreds of decks available, and here you'll get a sampling of over fifty different ones.

In this book there are lots of interesting things, including how you can use this book for divination. Bibliomancy is a form of divination that uses a book instead of, for example, a deck of cards. The Bible is probably the most commonly used book, but any book will do, even this one.

• EXERCISE 1 •

Bibliomancy

This exercise gives you an immediate introduction to at least one card. It is a stress-free way to do your first reading. Because the message may seem cryptic, it will also give you the opportunity to practice applying general interpretations to specific questions. It is also a fun and inspiring activity you can do whenever you want.

If you do not have a tarot deck or your deck isn't handy, use this book. Think of your question (such as *What do I need to know about* _____?), flip through chapters 3 and 4 in this book, and stop at any random page. The card on that page is your answer. Each card entry has an "instant answer," a pithy message from the card that you can apply to your question.

In addition to the instant answer, you can study the card image and read the rest of the text on that page, if you like. These quick and easy interactions are a great way to start learning about the cards.

Beyond using these pages for bibliomancy, you will find a bunch of other good stuff. You don't have to read the chapters in order. Feel free to dip in and out as your fancy strikes. Trust your curiosity and your intuition. Some of the topics include tarot history, symbolism and structure, tarot activities, the cards, and how to do readings.

After you read this book, if you are hungry for more, check out the further reading list for recommendations.

• • •

Glossary

Here is a list of words that may be either unfamiliar or used in a specific manner in this book:

Arcana: Arcana is from the Latin word for "secrets."

Court Cards: Court cards are found in each suit of the minor arcana. Each suit has its own page, knight, queen, and king. In some decks, these ranks are renamed. These cards represent people, aspects of someone's personality, or a role someone may play in a situation.

Cups: The suit of cups is a suit in a tarot deck, part of the minor arcana. This suit is sometimes called other names such as chalices or water. This suit deals with emotions, relationships, and creativity.

Divination: Divination is commonly thought of as seeing the future, although it can also mean communing with the Divine or seeking spiritual guidance.

Fortunetelling: Fortunetelling is the act of predicting or seeing the future.

Layout: See *Spread.*

Major Arcana: The major arcana is a section of a tarot deck. It contains twenty-two cards that have a name and a number, such as 0, the Fool; III (or 3), the Empress; XVI (or 16), the Tower, etc. As the major arcana, these cards represent tarot's greater secrets. These cards represent important life events and lessons, which are often circumstances beyond our control.

Minor Arcana: The minor arcana is a section of a tarot deck that contains fifty-six cards. It is further divided into four suits: wands, cups, swords, and pentacles. Each suit contains an ace through ten as well as four court cards. These cards represent the people and events of everyday life and are usually more within our control.

Pentacles: The suit of pentacles is a suit in a tarot deck and part of the minor arcana. This suit is sometimes called other names such as coins, stones, or earth. This suit deals with the physical world, material items, money, resources, and health.

Querent: A querent is the person in a tarot reading who is asking the question or getting the reading. If you are reading for yourself, you are the querent.

Reader: The reader is the person who interprets the cards in a reading.

Reading: A reading is the act of laying out the cards and interpreting them in order to get an answer to a question or to provide requested advice or guidance.

Reversal: Some people shuffle their decks so that the cards are not all facing the same way. They do this so that when they lay the cards in a spread, some will appear upright or in a normal position (that is, the top of the picture is at the top) and some will appear upside down (with the top of the picture at the bottom). These readers then incorporate the reversals into the reading, often giving those cards different meanings. Not all readers use reversals; it is not necessary to use them in order to be a good reader.

Spread: A spread, or layout, is a diagram or written description of how to lay out the cards in order to do a reading. Usually each position in a spread includes a description of what that position represents, such as "you," "the past," "the future," and "advice."

Swords: The suit of swords is a suit in a tarot deck and part of the minor arcana. This suit is sometimes called other names such as athames, knives, or air. This suit deals with reason, ways of thinking, and communication.

Tarot Deck: A tarot deck has seventy-eight cards. The cards divide naturally into two smaller parts: the major arcana and the minor arcana. Some decks call themselves tarot but may have more or fewer cards and may not have the same structure described here. Whether these decks are still considered a tarot deck is an area for intense debate amongst tarot users.

Wands: The suit of wands is a suit in a tarot deck and part of the minor arcana. This suit is sometimes called other names such as rods, batons, staffs, or fire. This suit deals with will, projects, career, and passion.

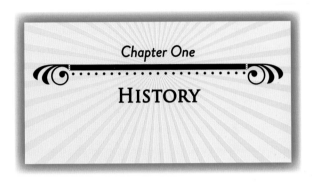

Chapter One

HISTORY

• • •

Most books about tarot include at least a little tarot history. Some people love history, while others couldn't care less. It's not necessary to know tarot history in order to read tarot. However, a little familiarity with tarot's story has one important benefit: it will help you understand how significantly tarot has changed over the years. This eliminates any concerns about "getting it wrong." Even a short look at tarot's history will illustrate that it has evolved and continues to evolve, and that, at the end of the day, there is no "right" or "wrong" way to work with the cards.

Although tarot constantly changes, one thing that has remained constant about the cards is the idea of stories. We humans love stories, and fortunately for us, tarot history is full of great stories. For example, tucked away in museums are a few decks that were created in the fifteenth century, miniature works of art dripping with gold leaf. These miniature works of art were sometimes commissioned as gifts. We know, for example, that in the mid-fifteenth century a deck was commissioned to celebrate the marriage of Francesco Sforza and Bianca Maria Visconti. It is said that some of the figures in the cards resemble the bride and the groom.

Another story is how at one time it was believed that the cards came from the pyramids in distant and mysterious Egypt, a gift from the Egyptian god Thoth given to humankind centuries ago but lost to obscurity. Luckily, a few eighteenth-century Europeans "rediscovered" this gift and gave it back to the world.

Some have said that the Gypsies (who were named after Egypt but were not actually from there) brought tarot cards to Europe, demanding that their palms be "crossed with silver." In exchange for the silver, they slowly turned over the cards, spinning tales of both fortune and woe.

Whether we think the stories are true or not is rather beside the point. They are still part of its history. They are part of why the tarot, after all this time, still holds the power to enchant and inspire us. Stories, fables, fairy tales, myths, jokes, movies…these are all ways we teach and learn lessons, ways we make sense of the world. And the cards themselves are used to tell stories. We shuffle the cards, lay them down, and we read them, just as we would a story. Are the stories we read in the cards any more or any less true than any other stories we tell? Perhaps they are all true in their own way. Because, really, the stories we tell say more about us than they do about the actual subject of the story. The line dividing truth, fact, and history from story, myth, and dream is not always clear.

The history most modern tarot scholars tell is based on available historical evidence, such as account books, receipts, laws, letters, and existing cards. Based on these sources, tarot cards were found in Europe in the fifteenth century. These hand-painted cards were used by noble families to play a card game called tarrochi, a trick-taking game similar to bridge. They were also given as gifts or to commemorate events (the Sforza-Visconti marriage story is actually true).

People started experimenting with tarot and fortune-telling in the eighteenth century, but it wasn't until the early twentieth century that tarot and divination really developed. In 1909 Arthur E. Waite published his deck with images painted by Pamela (Pixie) Colman Smith, now known as the Rider-Waite Tarot or Rider-Waite-Smith Tarot and one of the most important decks ever created. In 1943 Aleister Crowley and artist Lady Frieda Harris completed the Thoth Tarot, which wasn't published until 1969 and is still popular with readers. However, for whatever reason, the Rider-Waite-Smith Tarot (hereafter RWS) has become the standard deck, particularly in the United States. Most beginners learn with this deck, and the majority of decks published today are based on the RWS tradition, even though it was not the first tarot deck ever designed or even the first designed for divination.

Tarot's popularity really took off in the 1960s. Eden Gray's *The Tarot Revealed* and *Mastering the Tarot* became the first modern books about tarot. Eden Gray influenced many of today's most celebrated tarot authors, namely Rachel Pollack (*78 Degrees of Wisdom*) and Mary K. Greer (*Tarot for Your Self*).

Throughout the centuries, the images on the cards have changed. For example, the Strength card used to show a male figure reminiscent of Hercules beating a lion with a big club. The meaning of the card was using strength or force to control what was then considered our animal nature or impulses. Now it is more common to see a female character with the lion, gently opening or closing his mouth (it is usually purposefully ambiguous as to which). The interpretation in this case is about using a gentle, loving strength to encourage a desired behavior. Some more modern decks show the woman helping the lion in some way, pushing the interpretation even further toward accepting and healing our wounded parts, or what some call our shadow self. Even with this one example, we can see the history of human understanding.

From its birth during the Renaissance, tarot has entertained and delighted us. While the images and the way we use them have changed, the cards still manage to evoke a connection to the past and to the mysterious wisdom of the universe. Tarot is a path rich with entertainment, mystery, wisdom, and beauty, and each of us who ever shuffles a deck takes part in that ongoing journey, both shaping and being shaped by tarot.

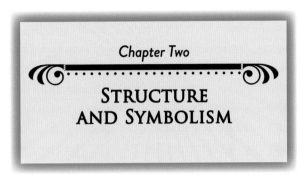

Chapter Two

STRUCTURE AND SYMBOLISM

• • •

You may have noticed that there are lots of oracle decks available, and perhaps you have wondered about the difference between tarot decks and oracle decks. Oracle decks are designed for divination, guidance, or inspiration. Not all oracle decks are tarot decks. What makes a tarot deck different? One thing that all tarot decks have in common is the structure.

Traditionally, a tarot deck has seventy-eight cards divided into two main parts, the major arcana and the minor arcana. There are twenty-two cards in the major arcana, numbered zero through twenty-one. Each major card has a number and a name. The name, along with the image, gives clues about the meaning of the card. For example, the Wheel of Fortune is about changes; the Chariot, about moving forward; Justice, about karma and consequences of actions; and the Devil, about unhealthy choices and behaviors. These cards represent important milestones or life events as well as lessons to be learned.

If you lay the major cards out in numerical order, you can see the Fool's journey. The Fool, numbered zero and representing starting out on a new adventure, travels through each of the other majors until he or she reaches the last card, the World, which represents the completion of a cycle. The Fool's journey is a fascinating way to explore the major cards, especially if you have an interest in mythology and the hero's journey.

The minor arcana breaks down into suits, like a regular playing card deck. Each suit has an ace through ten as well as four court cards named page, knight, queen, and king. Some people believe that the medieval courtly ranks are not relevant to modern society. Some decks rename these cards; for example, daughter, son, mother, father or student, seeker, sybil, and sage. The suits have common names, but there are sometimes variations. The suits (with variations in parentheses) are wands (rods, batons, staffs, fire), cups (chalices, water), swords (athames, knives, air), and pentacles (coins, stones, earth). While the majors have larger and more mythic implications, the minor cards represent the situations and people we encounter in our everyday lives.

In addition to structure, another component that makes tarot so intriguing is the use of symbols. Symbols are powerful images that mean more than the thing they depict. Over the past hundred years, tarot deck creators and authors have actively worked with traditional tarot symbols, changing, replacing, or eliminating them to make decks that are easier for us to connect with. Even still, though, there are some symbols that are very common in modern decks. In fact, there is one element from the RWS deck that wasn't intended as a symbol but became one. Pamela Colman Smith included a black cat in her painting for the Queen of Wands. The cat belonged to one of the people staying with her at the cottage where she worked on the deck. Most people these days say that the cat represents the keen intuition of the Queen of Wands, and most decks today include a black cat in this card.

Here are a few common symbols:

- Several cards have pillars or towers on either side of the central character, indicating balance or the middle path. Sometimes one pillar is white and the other black, showing the balance of opposing forces.

- Flowers can have meaning. White flowers, often lilies, are purity. Red flowers, usually roses, are passion. Yellow ones, such as sunflowers, are vitality and life. Flowers can be actual flowers or pictured on banners or flags.

- If a figure is wearing a crown or hat, it can represent what is on their mind or their top priority.

- When nudity is used in tarot, it usually means purity.

- Angels can mean divine messages.

- Birds are associated with thoughts and communication; butterflies, transformation.

When exploring a tarot deck, before researching symbols or reading what the deck creator intended, see for yourself what is going on in the image. Let your soul and your mind respond to what you see. Draw on any personal symbolism or what things mean to you. Form a personal connection with a deck.

The structure of the tarot deck helps make learning the cards easier by breaking the deck down into smaller, more manageable parts. Tarot has a lot of symbolism. Whether you prefer to take a systematic study approach or a more playful, hands-on one, tarot can potentially provide you with countless fascinating things to learn about yourself, your life, and the world around you.

Let's begin the real adventure now, shall we? Just turn the page to take the leap!

The Fool • Everyday Witch Tarot

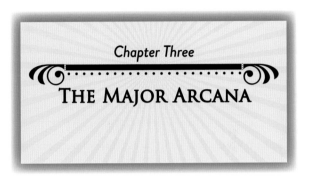

Chapter Three

THE MAJOR ARCANA

• • •

The major arcana cards represent important life events. Sometimes these events will be obvious turning points, such as enrolling in a course of study, getting married, getting divorced, moving, or releasing a behavior that no longer serves you. Not all life-changing events are obvious, though. If several major cards show up in a reading, even if it is about a seemingly mundane situation, pay attention. The question may have more significance than you imagined.

These cards are complex archetypes with richly nuanced meanings. For now, these short and sweet interpretations can give you guidance and inspiration. You can always explore further and go deeper into the cards. Before we begin to explore the major arcana, here is an exercise to help you form a personal relationship with a few of the majors.

Tarot Birth Cards

Calculating your tarot birth cards creates a personal connection with the cards. Your birth cards show your natural strengths, weaknesses, and areas of struggle. The card you are drawn to or like the most represents your strengths and areas of comfort. The other one illustrates your weaknesses. The relationship between the cards points to life lessons and areas of struggle in your life.

Birth cards come in pairs (and in one instance a set of three) and are connected numerologically. You calculate your birth cards by adding up the digits of your birthday. Keep reducing until you get a number that is under 21. To reduce a number, add the digits together. For example, my birth date is 1-16-1963. When I add those up, I get 1,980 (1 + 16 + 1963). To reduce, I add those digits to get 18, which is the number of the major arcana card called the Moon. Its corresponding card is 9, the Hermit, because when the digits of 18 are added together they equal 9 (1 + 8). You don't have to figure the corresponding card out, however; just find your initial birth card in the list below and you will find the matching card.

The groups of birth cards are:

10/1: Wheel of Fortune and Magician

11/2: Justice and High Priestess

12/3: Hanged Man and Empress

13/4: Death and Emperor

14/5: Temperance and Hierophant

15/6: Devil and Lovers

16/7: Tower and Chariot

17/8: Star and Strength

18/9: Moon and Hermit

19/10/1: Sun and Wheel and Magician

20/2: Judgement and High Priestess

21/3: World and Empress

Mucha Tarot

O · The Fool

KEYWORDS: *beginnings, innocence, spontaneity, adventure, faith, carelessness, eccentricity, apparent foolishness*

It is time for a fresh start. The Fool often comes up if you are at a crossroads. You may feel uncertain about the logistics of a certain choice, making this path feel like a foolish choice, but something in you is urging you forward. The Fool card lets you know that wherever your steps take you, you will have a wondrous adventure. The road may not always be easy, but in the end you will be able to celebrate an accomplishment that you can be proud of.

SYMBOLISM 1: *The Fool's Dog*

Most Fool images include a dog. Dogs represent faithfulness, devotion, and loyalty, as well as protection. As you step out into an uncertain future, the dog reminds you to have faith in yourself and your inner guidance. If you begin moving off your path, your internal compass will raise a fuss trying to get your attention, just like a barking dog warns of potential danger.

INSTANT ANSWER:
Take a deep breath and then take the leap!

THE MAGICIAN.

Rider-Waite Tarot

I · The Magician

KEYWORDS: *will, skill, manifestation, communication, magic, action, power, concentration, eloquence*

You have everything needed to create what you desire. The Magician's stance, one arm up and one arm down, shows the connection between higher guidance and manifesting reality. The tools on his table represent the elements of the universe that create the world we live in. The Magician used to represent a con man, so a little "fake it till you make it" attitude might be necessary.

JOURNAL PROMPT 1: *Beginning a Project*

Before beginning a project, think about what you want to accomplish. Compare it with your ideals and values. How well do they match up? What resources can you access? Be sure to consider how inspiration, logic, information, emotional support, and your personal network can fuel your endeavors.

INSTANT ANSWER:
Magic is will and preparation. The first step is knowing what you want.

Arcanum Tarot

II · The High Priestess

The High Priestess is the part of ourselves that is most connected with the Divine, our higher self, or our intuition. The moon and water imagery represent this deep thirst for something more, something mysterious. Listen to that quiet inner voice that so easily gets drowned out by the clutter of everyday life. Dreams, divination, and meditation are great ways to tune in. Turn your attention within and trust the way of knowing that is beyond logic.

SYMBOLISM 2: *The High Priestess*

The High Priestess is usually shown with a book or a scroll, representing inner wisdom that is not read with the eyes but with the soul. Her hands are folded in prayer, a way to connect with the Divine. The key has a small heart and a large heart, indicating that the discipline of inner seeking is the key to connecting your human heart with your divine heart.

INSTANT ANSWER:
You already know what to do. You don't need anyone else to validate your wisdom.

31

III • THE EMPRESS

III · The Empress

The quintessential earth mother, the Empress in tarot is not so much a political figure as she is an archetype in the cycle of life. In some images she may wear a crown and hold a scepter, but she is almost always shown at harvest time or with sheaves of wheat. She rules over the fertility and abundance of the world. She loves what she creates, finding its true beauty and nurturing it so that it can achieve its full potential. This card promises growth and prosperity.

JOURNAL PROMPT 2: *Mother Issues*

Some people do not like the Empress card and often cite issues with their own mother as the reason. If this is you, do not simply accept that you will never like or relate to this card. Instead of thinking about how you were mothered, focus on how you mother or care for the people, relationships, and things in your life. How can you learn to be a better mother in your life?

INSTANT ANSWER:
Generously do what you can to make the world a more loving, comfortable, beautiful place.

L'IMPERATORE · THE EMPEROR · DER HERRSCHER · EL EMPERADOR · L'EMPEREUR

IV

Nemo regere potest, nisi qui et regi

Tarot of Durer

IV · The Emperor

KEYWORDS: *stability, structure, authority, leadership, protection, stewardship, fatherhood, reason*

It is easy to confuse tarot's Emperor with modern-day political or economic control. The card shown here includes a quote from Seneca that says, "Moreover, there is no one who can rule unless he can be ruled," indicating the deeper meaning of the Emperor. Power and leadership are not for the ego but for the greater good. Managing resources and solving problems are key components to emperorship. When you get this card, consider your own authority and how you wield it.

TAROT TIP 1: *Card Pairs, Part 1*

One way to facilitate understanding some cards is to look at them as pairs. The Magician and High Priestess can represent two aspects of the self: the anima and animus, or the conscious and subconscious. The Empress and Emperor are another pair. The Empress provides what is needed to sustain life. The Emperor makes sure that bounty lasts through the winter.

INSTANT ANSWER:
Remember the fable about the ants and the grasshopper? Be the ants. Plan for the future.

Tarot of the Magical Forest

V · The Hierophant

The word *hierophant* comes from the Greek meaning to show or to make known, particularly in terms of sacred mysteries. The Hierophant is the teacher card. There is more to this card than sharing mundane knowledge, though. This card indicates expressing your most sacred values in your everyday life, wisdom that is more valuable than any degree. This card does not mean slavish devotion to ritual behavior. True tradition and ritual give stability and life.

SYMBOLISM 3: *The Keys*

The Hierophant is often shown with two keys crossed, referring to Jesus's words to Peter: "Whatever you bind on earth shall be bound in heaven, and whatever you loose on earth shall be loosed in heaven." This is another reminder that the Hierophant's most important job is to show us that our daily actions should be connected to our highest ideals.

INSTANT ANSWER:
Take the path of wisdom that adds to the stability and peace of the world.

37

THE LOVERS | VI | GLI AMANTI
LOS ENAMORADOS | | LES AMANTS

DIE LIEBENDEN | DE GELIEFDEN

Manga Tarot

VI · The Lovers

The original card was called the Lover and showed a man choosing between two women. The idea of choosing is still present in the card but is mingled with the desires of the heart. This card isn't just about romance or marriage, though. It is about making choices that are in line with your authentic heart. Some images show a sun and angel above the lovers, indicating that such a choice will be blessed and has life-giving qualities.

TAROT TIP 2: *Choices*

> Eliminate bias by writing your choices on pieces of paper. Fold the papers and mix them up so the words are hidden. Lay them out in a row. Pull three cards for each choice. Interpret them without knowing which choice they refer to. Make a decision (or at least an initial decision) based only on the cards. Then unfold the papers and see which is which.

INSTANT ANSWER:
Think about the person you really want to be. Make the choice that person would make.

VII – THE CHARIOT

VII – LE CHAR

Marseille Cat Tarot

VII · The Chariot

KEYWORDS: *drive, ambition, control, determination, success, movement, progress, speed, travel*

Images of the Chariot show a lot of potential power. The main figure wears a crown or helmet, showing strength, authority, or training, and carries a wand or scepter, another symbol of power. The sturdy chariot provides stability and protection. The creatures (these vary from deck to deck) are harnessed power at his fingertips, waiting to be used. But the chariot is usually not moving. Why? Because before setting that power into motion, you must know where you want to go.

JOURNAL PROMPT 3: *Growing Up*

> Some decks cleverly include one symbol from the first six major cards in the Chariot, representing the lessons learned in those first cards. What is the strongest characteristic you have from each of the first six cards? How have they helped you become a strong adult? How do they shape where you want to go and how you get there?

INSTANT ANSWER:
Power without self-control and discipline is just an accident waiting to happen. Know what you are doing and why you are doing it.

STRENGTH
LA FUERZA

ΧΙ

LA FORZA
LA FORCE

DIE STÄRKE

DE KRACHT

Tarot of the Sweet Twilight

VIII · Strength

KEYWORDS: *strength, gentleness, patience, compassion, healing, integration, courage*

There is something undeniably tender about a quiet, gentle person approaching a loud, potentially deadly creature without fear. Think of the woman as your higher self and the lion as your wounded or shadow self. Our wounded selves can cause havoc, especially when ignored or, even worse, denigrated. This card suggests that approaching your wounded self with kindness will heal you better than brute force.

TAROT TIP 3: *Create a Spread*

> Explore a card by creating a spread inspired by it. Use this card to investigate deep inner wounds. Draw a card to represent the woman/higher self, showing how to approach the issue. Pull a card to represent the lion and learn about the nature of the wound. Finally, pull a card to represent the origami Yoda to gain some wise insight.

INSTANT ANSWER:
Your gentle, courageous heart is your greatest strength. Follow its lead and see how powerful you are.

IX • THE HERMIT

Llewellyn's Classic Tarot

IX · The Hermit

KEYWORDS: *solitude, introspection, philosophy,
meditation, wisdom, guidance, privacy, isolation*

The Hermit is a state of being that we can all experience, and it is more than general introspection or simply wanting to be alone. The Hermit has gathered information, sometimes a lot of information. He then frees himself of distractions in order to sift through what he's learned. Comparing everything to his own heart and mind, he then draws conclusions and makes decisions. He uses this knowledge to fuel his lamp, which allows him to move through life with confidence.

TAROT TIP 4: *Hermit Time*

Hermit states can be of any duration. While it is lovely to fantasize about a long retreat to sort through our thoughts, most of us don't have that luxury. You can create hermit moments that fit easily into your life. Five minutes of meditation or a ten-minute journaling session can do wonders. Don't bring anything, especially the internet, to these precious times.

INSTANT ANSWER:
Spend time in the company of your soul.
Right now it is just what you need.

X The Wheel of Fortune

Anna.K Tarot

X · The Wheel of Fortune

KEYWORDS: *fortune, chance, cycle of life, opportunity, destiny, fate, luck, annual event*

Even though we have a lot of control in our lives, it is undeniable that sometimes random things happen. The Wheel of Fortune represents these often maddening but sometimes delightful (in which case we like to call it "serendipity") experiences. The wheel represents the hand of fate spinning the wheel of our lives, shaking things up and getting the energy moving. Most optimistic readers see this card as bringing a change for the better through a welcome bit of good luck.

SYMBOLISM 4: *Wheel of Fortune*

> The Wheel of Fortune is based on the Roman goddess Fortuna and her wheel. Many images have phrases near specific positions. At the top is "I rule." At the 3:00 spot is "I have ruled." Nine o'clock is "I will rule." The wheel itself represents the natural cycles of life, which often just flow. When Fortuna feels like playing, she'll spin the wheel—and that's when we get surprised.

INSTANT ANSWER:
Feeling lucky? Take the risk. Not feeling it? Don't. Whichever you do, hold on tight just in case.

11 · JUSTICE

Modern Spellcaster's Tarot

XI • Justice

KEYWORDS: *justice, karma, equality, truth, responsibility, integrity, fairness, contract, legal action*

Justice is the universal force that keeps the world in balance. Also known as karma, it is broader than the human legal system. Karmic justice usually takes longer, too. When this card comes up, think about what you are doing because it will have important consequences. It can also remind you that if you aren't happy with current circumstances, then you should review past behavior to see how you ended up in this pickle.

SYMBOLISM 5: *Justice and Consequences*

Not many Justice cards include a pomegranate, usually associated with abundance and fertility. It is an apt symbol for actions and consequences. When Persephone ate the pomegranate seeds, she had to face the consequences of staying in the underworld. The story also has an element of fairness, negotiation, and compromise, as Hades and Demeter eventually worked out a solution.

INSTANT ANSWER:
Today you are Justice. Your job: restore peace and balance in your little corner of the world.

XII

THE HANGED MAN

XII · The Hanged Man
• • • • • • • • • • • •

KEYWORDS: *letting go, sacrifice, surrender, restriction,*
delay, detachment, enlightenment, initiation

This card can mean sacrificing comfort (physical, mental, emotional, or spiritual) for enlightenment. It can also indicate a peaceful acceptance of what we cannot change. This image is a very modern depiction. Doing a yoga headstand requires discipline and practice, both forms of sacrifice, that brings benefits, both physical and mental. Seeing the world upside down forces us to see differently. Sometimes enlightenment can be as simple as seeing things from someone else's point of view.

JOURNAL PROMPT 4: *Sacrifice*

What are you willing to give up for what you want? What will you absolutely not sacrifice? How do you handle not being able to get what you want? Do you rail against the situation? Do you find a place of peaceful acceptance? What are the pros and cons of both these approaches? What can you gain? What do you lose? How do you determine when to quit fighting?

INSTANT ANSWER:
To see things more clearly, turn yourself
or the situation upside down and let
things come into surprising focus.

XIII Death

La Morte   Der Tod
La Mort   La Muerte

Fey Tarot

XIII · Death

KEYWORDS: *death, rebirth, endings, mortality,*
loss, change, transitions, transformation

This card rarely represents physical death. Whether physical death or some other major ending, this card involves loss and often mourning. Without Death, tarot would be an incomplete representation of the human experience. Without death and decay, there would be no seeds of new life nor space for future growth. When this card appears, major life changes are immanent. Embrace the whole experience, both the sense of loss and the hope of new life.

SYMBOLISM 6: *Death*

> This image has an eclipse on her chest, showing the inevitable diminishing of the sun along with the slowly returning light. The circular chess board is the circle of life. The king stands at the center, surrounded by the enemy, facing his certain demise, while Death watches and waits, patient and loving despite all her terrible power.

INSTANT ANSWER:
It is over, and there is no point trying to save it. Let it go with sorrow and gratitude, then turn your eyes to a brighter tomorrow.

TEMPERANCE
LA TEMPLANZA

XIV

LA TEMPERANZA
LA TEMPÉRANCE

DIE MÄSSIGKEIT

MATIGING

Lo Scarabeo Tarot

XIV · Temperance

KEYWORDS: *temperance, self-control, balance, moderation, harmony, synthesis, patience*

Temperance is maintaining your internal balance no matter the external circumstances, which requires constant self-adjustment as the environment changes. Think of a ballet dancer or yogini holding a pose. They look perfectly still, but hundreds of muscles are constantly working and adjusting to maintain the posture. This card reminds you that you may not be in control of the world around you, but you are in control of yourself.

JOURNAL PROMPT 5: *A Temperate Life*

> What does a balanced or moderate life mean to you? How do you structure your days in order to maintain balance? How do you react when something unexpected happens and you have to shuffle your plans? What is the relationship between flexibility and stability? How can you move through the world more gracefully?

INSTANT ANSWER:
Oak trees are awesome, but they are rigid.
Don't be an oak today.
Be a willow, flexible and elegant.

The Housewives Tarot

XV · The Devil

KEYWORDS: *bondage, obsession, materialism, temptation, doubt, lies, hopelessness, lack of options*

Most images of the Devil are surreal and terrifying, showing a great demon lording over unfortunate prisoners. This image is more playful and also more representative of modern views of the Devil card. Instead of selling our souls to demons, we sometimes destroy our own souls (and sometimes our lives) through unhealthy choices. This card asks us to consider the ways we are bound—and to find ways to free ourselves.

JOURNAL PROMPT 6: *Who Are Your Devils?*

What devils hold you in thrall? How did they come into your life? Were they little, mischievous imps to start? How did you make them comfortable (rearrange your life to accommodate them) and feed them, causing them to stay and grow large? What would you and your life be like without them? Do you ignore, excuse, or even love your devils?

INSTANT ANSWER:
Don't give in to temptation. In the end, you'll regret it. But if you do, forgive yourself and keeping trying to do better.

XVI

XVI

Hip Witch Tarot

XVI · The Tower

KEYWORDS: sudden change, upheaval, downfall, destruction, chaos, release, awakening, escape

The Tower represents our worldview. We spend a lot of time creating it, and it is the foundation of how we live our lives. As we change, our worldviews must change. If we do not alter them, then the universe steps in to help us out. A sudden disruption cracks the now-faulty edifice to pieces. While it is pretty messy, it is a gift. All the outmoded, unhealthy, and inappropriate ideas, structures, and relationships are swept away, leaving plenty of space to build anew.

SYMBOLISM 7: The Tower

> The witches' hats are falling off, showing how it is easy to lose focus during a Tower experience. The lightning is an unexpected destructive force that also illuminates. The exploding mountain, assumed to be a solid foundation, falls apart. The monkshood represents the feelings experienced: stimulation in the form of freaking out, followed by paralysis and disbelief.

INSTANT ANSWER:
Hold on to your hat and expect the unexpected. It just might be a bumpy ride.

XVII · *The Star*

Mystic Faerie Tarot

XVII · The Star

KEYWORDS: *hope, faith, healing, cleansing, guidance, peace, blessing, wishes*

Stars are associated with guidance. Ships navigate by the stars, and we sometimes call our guiding principles our North Star. The three wise men followed a star to find the Prince of Peace. We wish upon stars, asking them to bring us our hearts' deepest desires. When this card comes up, it promises a space of gentle comfort where we are healed and our faith is restored. If we are in need of forgiveness, the Star offers that, too. After tragedy, we find peace.

JOURNAL PROMPT 7: *Forgiveness*

Forgiveness can be hard. We may hold grudges or demand fair retribution for wrongs done to us. Withholding forgiveness, whether we are asked for it or not, is a cruel act. The Star is associated with both forgiveness and healing, indicating a connection. Forgiveness is part of the healing process. What are you not forgiving in yourself, and what healing is that blocking?

INSTANT ANSWER:
You want guidance and renewal? Give it!
Be a walking blessing. Smile, comfort,
and encourage others. You may find all
that goodness reflected back at you.

THE MOON
LA LUNA

XVIII

LA LUNA
LA LUNE

DER MOND

DE MAAN

Initiatory Tarot of the Golden Dawn

XVIII · The Moon

KEYWORDS: *secrets, deception, subconscious, confusion, cycles, dreams, nightmares, psychic ability*

In real life the moon is beguiling, enchanting, mysterious, and inspiring, but the Moon card has a dark side. This card can indicate dreams, psychic experiences, or even cycles, and there are other cards that represent those. The Moon card indicates illusion and deception. By its light everything is shadowy and blurry. The moon hides and distorts as much as it reveals. When this card appears, delay making decisions and wait for the light of day, or you could lose your way.

SYMBOLISM 8: **The Moon**

> The Moon card is rich in symbolism. The water represents the subconscious, and the lobster or crayfish emerging from it is our deepest fears. There is usually a domesticated dog (internal fears) and a wild dog or wolf (external fears). The path is the way through fear and confusion. The two towers mark a threshold of a place beyond fear, or at least beyond the current fear.

INSTANT ANSWER:
If something is too good (or bad) to be true, it probably is. In this case it's okay to verify first and trust second.

THE SUN

FIRE LEO   **19**   THE SUN

Next World Tarot

XIX · The Sun

KEYWORDS: happiness, joy, optimism, confidence, enthusiasm, clarity, success, celebration, vitality

The sun gives light and life to the earth. Symbolically, it is also the light of conscious understanding. Clarity makes it easy to feel confident and optimistic. We feel energized and ready to express ourselves. We are a little in love with ourselves and the entire world. When this card comes up, expect to feel great and to find enjoyment in everything (or even in just doing nothing).

TAROT TIP 5: *Yearly Reading*

> Doing readings is a great way to mark holidays, particularly your birthday. Put one card in the center to mark the general theme of your year, then put twelve cards around it, one for each month of the year. Keep track of the cards and revisit them at the beginning and end of the relevant month.

INSTANT ANSWER:
Throw a party—just because
life is so amazing and you feel good.
By the way, you look lovely!

XX · Judgement

Tarot in Wonderland

XX · Judgement

KEYWORDS: *rebirth, renewal, calling, awakening, decision, forgiveness, redemption, absolution*

Judgement is such a misunderstood card, and the title distracts from the true message. This card is really about responding to something that breathes new life into one that may feel dead or stagnant. Usually this card shows dead bodies being called to life…death in boxes changed to vibrant bodies ready to express their true soul's purpose. We reach toward the idea that there must be something more to life and yearn to become our best selves.

JOURNAL PROMPT 8: *Rebirth*

> The Judgement card usual has an angel (or other being) sounding a trumpet to wake up the dead. If you are being called to something new by a higher being, presumably it is toward something better. Can you be your own angel? Can you identify dead areas in your life that can be transformed into something fresh?

INSTANT ANSWER:
Your future self is calling.
Don't let it go to voicemail.

XXI

The World

Mystical Manga Tarot

XXI · The World

KEYWORDS: *completion, success, accomplishment, fulfillment, endings/beginnings, celebration, travel*

It's been a long and eventful journey with plenty of challenges overcome, lessons learned, and blessings received. This is a card of completion and achievement. Like all endings, it is also the mark of a new beginning—but don't turn your eyes too soon to the next adventure. Spend some time basking in your victory and celebrate with friends. These moments are rare enough, so don't rush past them.

TAROT TIP 6: *The Fool's Journey*

> This is an interesting way to study the major arcana. Place the Fool at the top, then arrange the cards in order in three rows of seven cards each. The first row represents learning how to function in society. The second row questions all the assumptions learned in the first row. The last row illustrates the path of spiritual growth.

INSTANT ANSWER:
Forget "just do it"...you've done it.
Take off your running shoes and soak
in a long hot bath. You earned it.

KING OF CUPS

◆

Otherkin Tarot

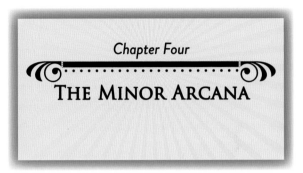

Chapter Four

THE MINOR ARCANA

• • •

Over two-thirds of the cards in a tarot deck are in the minor arcana. The major cards are beguiling and exciting, full of big changes and turns of fortune. Most of life, however, is made up of the small, ordinary things we do in a day. These minor cards may not be as fancy as the majors, but without them the tarot could not accurately portray all aspects of the human experience. Within the four suits of the minor arcana are the faces of love, hate, abundance, lack, ambition, ennui, ideas, and obsessions. In addition to these experiences, there are sixteen court cards representing the people who fill our lives, both intimately and casually.

Because these cards mark moments and situations of everyday life, they are not as complex as the majors. Even so, there is still a lot to learn about each one. Cards showing problems also contain the keys to solving those problems. Images representing happier times include ideas for nurturing more good times. The trick with the minor cards is not overthinking them while at the same time not undervaluing them.

Court cards are shown as male or female, but note that they can represent either gender. Gender is symbolic in the tarot, not literal. Also, apparent age is symbolic. A page, for example, may be a younger person or someone who feels young or inexperienced in the situation being looked at in the reading.

Wands

The suit of wands is associated with the element of fire. Thinking about fire helps us understand this suit. Fiery passions, heated tempers, relentless drive...these are all part of the suit of wands. More than anything, wands are associated with our will, our desire to express our unique selves in the world. Because of this, wands are often associated with careers and projects. This association has probably been strengthened because in America what we do for a living largely describes who we are and how important we are. But let's remember that we are more than our jobs and that wands are also about creativity and confidence, about making choices in line with our authentic selves, and about managing our egos. Being yourself and living authentically in the world requires boldness and courage. Luckily, the wands represent those exciting qualities as well.

The wands court cards are all considered to be very confident, charismatic, and attractive (whether in appearance or personality). They are exciting to be around and inspire action. Because wands are connected to fire, they are associated with the fire signs in astrology: Aries, Leo, and Sagittarius.

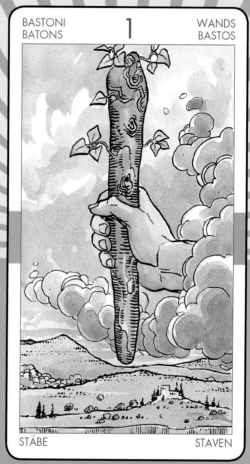

BASTONI
BATONS

1

WANDS
BASTOS

STÄBE

STAVEN

Universal Tarot

Ace of Wands

KEYWORDS: *passion, will, drive, inspiration, potency, energy, confidence, courage, optimism*

The Ace of Wands is like a fully loaded magic wand or a divine thumbs-up. While the opportunity may seem small, it holds a lot of energy and possibility. It will set your enthusiasm, inspiration, and creativity on fire. If you are looking for a project that ignites your drive and passion, the Ace of Wands is exactly what you want. But move quickly; the aces represent a small window of opportunity.

TAROT TIP 7: *Card Pairs, Part 2*

As you do more readings—especially if you keep track of and review your readings—you will begin noticing that pairs or groups of cards will start repeating. Pay attention to them and see if these pairs or groups mean something. For example, some readers say that the Empress and the Ace of Wands represent pregnancy.

INSTANT ANSWER:
Yes.

Pagan Cats

Two of Wands

KEYWORDS: *vision, determination, intention, confidence, business or career proposal or decision*

Possibility abounds as far as your eyes can see. It's almost embarrassing how many ideas you have and how many things you want to create. Having lots of options is supposed to be a blessing, right? Like all the twos, the Two of Wands is not about the nature of the choices but about how to make the choice. There are lots of ways to make a decision. The message here is to rely on your will, passion, and courage to guide you rather than on logic, emotions, or outcome.

TAROT TIP 8: *Easy vs. Hard Choices*

> Hard decisions aren't necessarily about important things. A difficult decision is one where there is no clear best choice. To help make the decision, use the twos. Pull them out of your deck, shuffle, and draw one. The Two of Wands advises relying on passion and courage; cups, emotions and relationship; swords, logic and common sense; pentacles, the desired outcome or finances.

INSTANT ANSWER:
If an opportunity doesn't make you say
"Hell yes!" immediately, then just say no.

3 OF WANDS

Mystic Dreamer Tarot

Three of Wands

KEYWORDS: *optimism, expectation, culmination, the law of attraction, return on investment*

The Three of Wands invites you to put your plans into motion. Make your investments, put in the orders, open up shop. This card involves a lot of activity—but that's the easy part. The image shows the hard part: waiting. After you've done all you can do, you have to wait for your ship to come in. Your attitude while waiting matters. Wands are about confidence, so shine that out into the world and attract the best possible results.

TAROT TIP 9: *Telling a Story*

Reading tarot is about more than memorizing individual card meanings. Practice reading the cards as a group. One way is to lay out the ace through ten of a suit. Look at the images and see how one relates to the next and how together they tell a unified story. You can begin with the wands since you now already have a head start for the ace, two, and three.

INSTANT ANSWER:
Keep your eyes peeled! Something
you worked for is bearing fruit.

Forest of Enchantment Tarot

Four of Wands

KEYWORDS: *holiday, party, celebration,
award ceremony, communal achievement*

The Four of Wands marks a special occasion. Whether it is an achievement or an unexpected blessing, this card reminds you of the importance of celebrating milestones. If the situation is worth noting, it is worth some planning and preparation. Besides, sometimes it is nice to use the good china, light some candles, and prepare some special food and drink. Gather your friends and have a good time. There will be time enough for work afterwards, starting with the cleaning up.

SYMBOLISM 9: *Numbers*

> Numbers are symbols, and fours represent stability. The wands and swords benefit from four's slowness. The fiery energy of wands is contained, and in the swords the chaotic energy of our thoughts finds rest. The cups and pentacles are already slow. The water of the cups grows swampy, and the earthy energy of the pentacles stops flowing entirely and becomes possessive.

INSTANT ANSWER:
Accept any social invitations. If none are forthcoming, issue your own invitations.

5

WANDS

Five of Wands

KEYWORDS: *competition, conflict, committees, strong personalities, differing opinions, lack of leadership*

Working in a group isn't always easy. The number five is inherently chaotic, so a competition that might bring out the best in people can quickly turn combative. Wills clash, disagreements abound. People might lose sight of the goal and become fixated on their own agendas. Bring calming energy to the situation to get back on track. This doesn't only occur when working with others; sometimes we fight with ourselves. When you feel frazzled, slow down and refocus.

SYMBOLISM 10: *Salamanders*

> The wands are associated with fire, and lots of decks include salamanders on the wands, especially on the court cards. These are mythical salamanders, ones that can pass through fire without being harmed. Sometimes in the wands we are asked to face a trial by fire, which requires courage.

INSTANT ANSWER:
Check your ego at the door and
keep your goal in mind.

Six of Wands

Everyday Witch Tarot

Six of Wands

KEYWORDS: *victory, honor, achievement, recognition, pride, public ceremony, success, triumph*

The Six of Wands promises success in an endeavor, and with that often comes public recognition. This card also brings a lesson. All heroes are part of a community that helps prepare and support the hero. Accept the honor with grace and generosity. Share the spotlight and rewards with those who made it possible. There is plenty of good feeling to spread around. In fact, the more who partake, the more there seems to be.

JOURNAL PROMPT 9: *Scarcity Mentality*

> Just as we can fall prey to scarcity mentality with money, we can also have a scarcity mentality about recognition. A strong, healthy ego knows the benefits of sharing. How do you respond to recognition or even compliments? How are you at giving recognition or compliments? When was the last time you shared an honor that you received?

INSTANT ANSWER:
You did it!
Own it and walk proudly.

7

Fairy Lights Tarot

Seven of Wands

KEYWORDS: *defending, protecting, valor, courage, standing up for beliefs, resolve, taking action*

Sometimes you feel like things are coming at you relentlessly and just won't stop. We've all gone through phases like that, and there are various ways to deal with those times. Laying low is one way. The Seven of Wands, though, says that you should stand up and face the onslaught with courage and confidence. Be clear on your values. Once you activate your will and express your intent, you can get things flowing in a more orderly and manageable way.

TAROT TIP 10: *Prioritizing*

When we try to manage too many things, we need to take a breath, settle down, and prioritize. List out your tasks. Pull a card for each of them. Using the numbers on the cards, make an orderly list. If there are repeat numbers, use the suits to further order them: wands, cups, swords, and pentacles. If you get a court card, that is something to delegate.

INSTANT ANSWER:
Stand up and take charge. You got this.

Eight of Wands

Animal Totem Tarot

Eight of Wands

*KEYWORDS: speed, travel, messages,
things running smoothly, expected result*

If the Eight of Wands turns up, the message is clear: things will turn out exactly as they were designed to. That is, events that have been set in motion will reach their logical outcome. If you planned well, things will move quickly in the right direction. What if the direction is not what you want? With things moving so fast, changing things will create chaos, so it might be wiser to let things play out and deal with the consequences when things are calmer.

TAROT TIP 11: *Resetting Your Deck*

If your readings feel confused, try resetting your deck by putting your cards in order. Most people use this order: major arcana, 0–21 first, followed by the suits: wands, cups, swords, and pentacles, ace–ten, page, knight, queen, king. Then you get the great pleasure of shuffling a lot in order to re-randomize your cards.

INSTANT ANSWER:
Dot your i's and cross your t's because
the details will matter a lot very soon.

Mystic Wizards Tarot

Nine of Wands

KEYWORDS: *protecting, defending, stamina, loyalty, strength, discipline, wounded warrior*

You've been fighting long and well, but you're still not quite done. Even though that's not what you want to hear, you probably knew it in your gut. There are people counting on you, and you are counting on yourself. You are committed to the cause and couldn't stop now, even if you wanted to. The good news is that you do have the courage, stamina, and strength to see this through.

TAROT TIP 12: *Personal Anecdotes*

When reading for others, use personal anecdotes that describe how the card's message applies in real life. When were you weary from handling too much for too long? What helped you? What fueled you? How did things end, and how did you feel afterwards? How can you relay that story concisely so that you can tell it when needed? This is a good exercise to do for all the cards.

INSTANT ANSWER:
Even running on fumes, you are more powerful than you know. Trust your inner fire.

Ten of Wands

Mystic Faerie Tarot

Ten of Wands

. . . .

KEYWORDS: *burdens, obligations, numerous opportunities, duties, responsibilities*

Sometimes we are so inspired that we say yes to everything. Eventually all the things that thrilled us become burdens or obligations. Now instead of being fueled by an inner fire, we can barely manage the external fires we created. The Ten of Wands doesn't just describe the situation but offers advice. You don't have to keep doing it all. It's okay to admit that something isn't working or isn't fulfilling. Set some things aside and select a few to focus on.

SYMBOLISM 11: *A Heavy Load*

> In the Ace of Wands in this deck, the boy sets out to find a dragon. Throughout the cards he studies dragon care, acquires an egg, and eventually gets a dragon. He achieved his goal, but it was more than he could handle. The result is that he is in a situation that isn't good for him or the dragon. What we want isn't always good for us. Knowing when to let go is a kind of wisdom.

INSTANT ANSWER:
Don't burn the candle at both ends
or you'll go up in flames.

PAGE ⊕F WANDS

Celtic Tarot

Page of Wands

KEYWORDS: *young or inexperienced person,*
supporter, energy, creativity, sensitive ego

Pages are young or inexperienced. Pages of Wands want to do, do, do, and having to wait or hold back makes them impatient. Their weaknesses include a fragile ego and a possibly volatile nature. They are embarrassed easily, leading to defensiveness or anger. Treat them kindly with lots of patience until they gain confidence. If you do, you will have gained a supporter. If you don't, you may have to spend time and energy dealing with the fallout.

SYMBOLISM 12: *Animal Companions*

Court card images often include animal companions that give a hint about the person's nature. This page has a dragon draped over her, representing her innate fiery energy. It isn't threatening, but it is threatening to engulf her, meaning that it is controlling her rather than her being in control of it. Pages do have a lot of power, but they don't always know how to use it.

INSTANT ANSWER:
You can do this, but it may take a few tries.
Be patient with yourself and
the learning process.

KNIGHT OF WANDS   CAVALIERE DI BASTONI
CABALLO DE BASTOS   CHEVALIER DE BÂTONS

RITTER DER STÄBE   STAVEN RIDDER

Lo Scarabeo Tarot

Knight of Wands

KEYWORDS: *focused, short attention span, charming, bully, strong ego, honorable, courageous*

Knights are focused and have experience but lack authority. The Knight of Wands applies his confidence, honor, and courage—and incredible charm—to achieve his goal. He may ignore the needs of others or bully others to do what he wants. Appeal to his ego, honor, or courage to help him channel his energy in a useful direction. If not, lay low and let him do his thing. Luckily, he often has a short attention span and will eventually direct his energy elsewhere.

SYMBOLISM 13: *Knight of Wands*

This knight has a salamander on his chest that is almost eating its tail. This indicates a more complete integration of the fiery wands energy. He is riding a lion, a symbol of his courage. Pay attention to things on people's heads, as they can indicate what is on their mind or their guiding principle. In this case, the red plume represents his passion and will.

INSTANT ANSWER:
Your word for today is "focus." Give all your attention to the thing that needs doing and don't stop until it's done.

Queen of Wands

Pagan Otherworlds Tarot

Queen of Wands

KEYWORDS: *confidante, accomplished, decisive, impatient, dramatic, charismatic, loves attention*

The queens have knowledge, experience, and authority and are concerned with individual or small group connections. The Queen of Wands is incredibly confident and charming, with keen intuition. She takes action, makes decisions, and can be a wonderful leader. She can be impatient, especially with fools or indecisive people. While her vibrant personality naturally draws others to her, she will take steps to keep attention on her if she feels it wandering.

SYMBOLISM 14: *Sunflowers and Cats*

> Originally the Queen of Wands was shown with a tiger, but the RWS illustrator, Pamela Colman Smith, changed all that when she substituted her model's pet cat for the tiger. Ever since, almost every queen is shown with a black cat, which is said to represent her intuition. The sunflower marks her connection to the fiery energy of the sun.

INSTANT ANSWER:
Shine brightly, confident in your glorious self!

Fire Alpha Male

Magical Dogs Tarot

King of Wands

KEYWORDS: *decision-maker, power, experience, action, decisive, seeks excitement and adventure*

Kings have knowledge, experience, and authority and are concerned with large group and infrastructure/organizational situations. The King of Wands loves action and starting new projects and dislikes bureaucracy and committees. Gain his support with exciting ideas appealing to his sense of adventure and avoid boring or embarrassing him. He is brave and committed to his ideals, so even without popular support, he will do what he thinks is right.

TAROT TIP 13: *Be a Leader*

> Even for those who like learning alone, exchanging ideas with others keeps your practice lively. Practicing with other tarot lovers means you get to do readings but also can get deeper feedback on your techniques and interpretations. If there isn't a tarot group in your area (check social media platforms and local metaphysical stores), consider being brave and starting one.

INSTANT ANSWER:
You have the chance to make something wonderful happen if you apply your amazing personality and skills.

THREE OF CUPS

Fairy Tale Tarot

Cups

The suit of cups is associated with the element of water. Thinking about water helps us understand this suit. Watery weeping jags, relationships that threaten to drown us, and deep secrets are all part of the suit of cups. More than anything, cups are associated with our emotions, our desire to know and be known, and our need to connect. Emotions are so challenging sometimes. Other times, they are what make life worth living. The suit of cups reminds us that all emotions are part of life. Like ships riding on a stormy ocean, it is all too easy to be tossed about by our feelings, losing control, going under. Emotional maturity allows us to swim instead of sink. This suit helps us navigate the sometimes painful path to emotional maturity as well as celebrate the most joyous moments in our lives.

The cups court cards are usually sensitive, empathetic, and loving souls. They value connection and community. They can also, oddly enough, be solitary creatures, getting lost in their daydreams. The cups courts are usually the artists of the deck, happy to be behind the scenes, behind the lens, or working in a studio. The cups court cards are associated with the water signs in astrology: Pisces, Cancer, and Scorpio.

ACE OF CHALICES

Silver Witchcraft Tarot

Ace of Cups

The Ace of Cups is like receiving a magic potion full of healing, grace, and peace. You can think of it as a personal Holy Grail, a beautiful offering of exactly what your heart and soul need. You are invited to drink deeply, quenching that mysterious thirst and filling your own well. This allows you not only to feel whole, but it also spreads to others as you share your gift. But move quickly; the aces represent a small window of opportunity.

TAROT TIP 14: *Exalting Aces*

When laying out a spread, take any ace out of its spot, place it at the top of the reading, and draw a new card for the empty space. The aces add focus. Wands focuses on career, projects, and things you want to do; cups focus on emotions, intimacy, and relationships; swords focus on communication, thought processes, and ideas of truth; and pentacles focus on finances, resources, and health.

INSTANT ANSWER:
Bottoms up! Fill your well so you always have enough to share.

CHALICES
COPAS

2

COPPE
COUPES

KELCHE

BEKERS

Tarot of the Sweet Twilight

Two of Cups

KEYWORDS: *partnership, connection, falling in love, harmony, kindred spirit, attraction*

There are all types of love you can fall into. Romance could be in the air and you may meet eyes with a stranger and everything clicks. You might meet a new friend or discover a new author or new hobby. In those instances, you have to make a choice: pursue this or not. There is no guarantee of anything except a wonderful romp for your heart. Things don't have to last forever to be successful. Let go of expectations and explore the wondrous possibilities.

TAROT TIP 15: *Relationships*

Romance is one of the most popular subjects for readings. If you are interested in seeing the potential of a new relationship, pull three cards for yourself and three cards for the other person, laying them side by side. See if there are areas of compatibility or ones of potential conflict. You can pull more cards for advice on managing areas of potential conflict.

INSTANT ANSWER:
Today your heart gets to make the decisions.

Three of Cups

Tarot in Wonderland

Three of Cups

KEYWORDS: *friendship, family, casual parties, fun, abandon, connections, savoring the moment*

Being with people you are most comfortable with is both relaxing and energizing. Your similarities with your friends connects you. Your differences enhance each other's best qualities. Even though simply being with these people can feed your soul, casual gatherings are often low priority in our busy lives. The Three of Cups reminds you to value your friends and make time to be together.

JOURNAL PROMPT 10: *Best Friends*

> Who are your best friends? How do you feel when you are with them? What do you value most in them? What do they value in you? Do they help you grow as a person? How do you support and help them? After hanging out, do you feel stronger or diminished? If diminished, what are you getting from the relationship? Is it time to find new friends?

INSTANT ANSWER:
Girls' (or boys') night out!

Four of Cups

Everyday Witch Tarot

Four of Cups

This card is filled with ennui and dissatisfaction. You don't like what you have, but you haven't the heart or the energy to try something new. It is all so hard! Why is life so boring and awful? We all have times like this, and it is okay to recognize and feel your feelings. The danger with this card is in getting stuck. Even if you don't feel like it, wash your face, put on clean clothes, and visit the outside world. The cat in this card knows that curiosity keeps life exciting.

JOURNAL PROMPT 11: *Boredom*

> Define boredom. Can boredom be a mask for other issues like procrastination, avoidance, or fear? How do you handle boredom? When does boredom strike? What methods are best to shake you out of this state? Are there benefits to experiencing boredom? Is boredom necessary, at least for periods of time, to create space for fresh inspiration?

INSTANT ANSWER:
You get ten minutes to wallow, then go take a shower and wash all that muck away. Go out and do something new. Smile at a stranger.

Five of Cups

Mermaid Tarot

Five of Cups

KEYWORDS: *mourning, grief, feelings of loss, sadness, regret, repentance, bitterness, frustration*

The Five of Cups is about true mourning. Grief is what we feel after a great loss; mourning is the outward expression of grief. Our culture isn't big on mourning and will encourage you to get over it. The trick is finding the balance between repressing your grief and overindulging it. Make space for your feelings. Find someone who can honor your emotions and sit with you while you process them without trying to fix you.

SYMBOLISM 15: *Grief*

The three toppled cups are the loss, and the two upright cups are what remains. The structure in the distance represents the return to what we would call a "normal" life. Of course, nothing will ever be the same again, but you will adjust your actions, thoughts, and feelings to accommodate holes created by loss and to make room for the new realizations the experience brought you.

INSTANT ANSWER:
Find a sympathetic friend and hold on tight until the rough waters of your soul are quieted.

6

CHALICES

Six of Cups

This card highlights the significance of small, quiet moments. Through simple acts of kindness, selfless generosity, and sweet words, we build connections and memories with others. Honoring these ties helps us remember that we are all one. We all suffer, are wounded, have bad days, make bad choices, and say stupid things. Those things can really divide us unless we have nurtured our connections. The Six of Cups invites you to indulge in happy memories or making new ones.

TAROT TIP 16: *Negative Meanings*

Some of the keywords listed are negative because all the cards have a range of meaning. For example, sweet memories can warm your heart and aid in forgiveness. However, humans can really rewrite history in ways that negatively affect the present. Romanticizing a past experience will make it harder for any present experience to measure up.

INSTANT ANSWER:
Commit random acts of kindness.

Seven of Cups

Mermaid Tarot

Seven of Cups

KEYWORDS: *confusion, fantasies, choices, imagination, dreams, lack of focus, wishful thinking*

No choices can be as hard as too many choices. The Seven of Cups brings lots of possibilities, some realistic, some fantasy, some healthy, some dangerous. This card shows up when you are drowning in dreams. Which cup should you reach for? Dreams can turn into goals if you pick the right one and start doing the work to make it real. Unrealistic fantasies can sap your time and energy (and resources). Too many dreams can keep you from taking action in the real world.

TAROT TIP 17: *Elemental Advice*

When you are dealing with a card that doesn't seem to have advice built in, try bringing in another elemental energy. The Seven of Cups shows possibilities but no real advice for knowing how to decide. Because the suit of cups is passive, try incorporating an active energy. The logic of swords can help divide the achievable dreams from the time wasters.

INSTANT ANSWER:
Let your imagination go wild! Dream all the great things. Reality will be there when you get back.

8   Chalices

Coppe   Kelche
Coupes   Copas

Fey Tarot

Eight of Cups

Have you ever had the feeling that something is missing,
even though things are pretty good and nothing is actually
wrong? But in your heart, you know things won't ever be
right until you figure out that missing piece. What makes
it harder is that the yearning comes from your heart and
often isn't easily expressed in words. It's not easy to leave
a comfortable, pleasant situation, but the longer you
ignore your heart, the more uncomfortable it will be to
stay.

TAROT TIP 18: *What Your Heart Wants*

> Most readings use randomly drawn cards, symbolizing
> the chaos and chance of life. But we also have
> the power to make choices. Go through the deck
> faceup and pick all cards that deeply touch your
> heart in this moment. Narrow those choices to 3–5
> cards. Weave them together to create your answer
> to this question: What does my heart want?

INSTANT ANSWER:
You might not know what you are
looking for. Don't worry. Your heart will
let you know when your eyes see it.

NINE OF CUPS

Vivid Journey Tarot

Nine of Cups

KEYWORDS: *wishes fulfilled, satisfaction with life, pride, hospitality, worldly pleasures, happiness*

The Nine of Cups is traditionally known as the "wish card." Before beginning a reading, the reader asks the querent to make a wish. If, during the course of the reading, the Nine of Cups comes up, it means the wish will come true. This card describes someone who is content with their life, emotionally satisfied, and feeling pretty good about themselves and the world in general. Life isn't always this carefree, so enjoy this time and give thanks for the blessings.

JOURNAL PROMPT 12: *You as the Nine of Cups*

> The image in a card often reflects the deck creator's own ideas about a card. The figure in this card sometimes has crossed arms, showing that he wants to keep all the goodness for himself. Other decks show the figure with open arms, meaning he prefers to share his blessings. If you were to be your own Nine of Cups figure, would your arms be opened or closed? Why?

INSTANT ANSWER:
Make a wish!
The universe is ready to grant it.

10

Ten of Cups

. . . .

KEYWORDS: *family, domestic bliss, comfort,*
peace, sanctuary, happiness, deep affection

The Ten of Cups indicates that your relationships are a
safe space where you can wash away the cares of the day
and remember the goodness in the world. This card is like
a "they lived happily ever after" situation but even better, with deep commitment and very real affection. Those
characteristics keep you together through good times and
tough times. They help us not give up on each other and
give us strength to live our best lives.

TAROT TIP 19: *Dedicated Decks*

Some people dedicate different decks to different
types of readings: love, career and finances,
spiritual exploration. If you work with crystals,
use them to focus or dedicate your deck to a
specific purpose. A deck for love can be stored
with rose quartz; finances, citrine; spiritual,
amethyst. If you don't have dedicated decks, use
an appropriate crystal on your reading table.

INSTANT ANSWER:
Love is all you need—and some
people to share it with.

PAGE OF CUPS

Otherkin Tarot

Page of Cups

KEYWORDS: *message, youth, inexperience, supporter, curiosity, sensitive, needy, romantic, sweet*

Pages are young or inexperienced. The Page of Cups longs to dive into the deep and sometimes turbulent waters of relationship. He is in love with being in love. He is sensitive, sweet, and loving. He can be needy, clingy, and prone to secretiveness. Guide him with kindness, teach him about boundaries, and nurture his dreams so that he retains his good nature and doesn't become cynical. If you do so, you will have a devoted friend.

TAROT TIP 20: *Pages as Messages*

Pages were traditionally associated with messages, which is why you sometimes see references to letters in some images, such as this one. The page's suit indicates what the message will be about. The Page of Cups might deliver a love letter; swords, news about a legal case or decision; wands, a career offer; and pentacles, information about a loan, a raise, or a bill.

INSTANT ANSWER:
Write a love letter to someone dear to you—not a text but a proper letter sent through the mail. Don't forget to seal it with a kiss.

KNIGHT OF CUPS

Tarot of the Hidden Realm

Knight of Cups

KEYWORDS: *focused, goal-oriented, short attention span, dreamer, committed, idealistic, romantic*

Knights are focused and have experience but lack authority. The Knight of Cups devotedly quests for his heart's desire. He is more of a dreamer than a doer, loving beauty and valuing ideals. Don't expect him to be something he is not, such as a good leader or a "take charge" type of person. To gain his support, show him how your cause really helps someone in need or serves a greater ideal. He needs something or someone worthwhile to serve, otherwise he is lost.

JOURNAL PROMPT 13: *How You Serve*

> We have aspects of all the courts within us. The knights are about service. The Knight of Cups is in service to his heart; wands, to his ego; swords, to the truth; and pentacles, to stewardship. How do you express each of these? If any of the knights is missing from you, how could you cultivate them? Are any of your inner knights in service to something contrary to your values?

INSTANT ANSWER:
Find joy in being of service.

QUEEN OF CUPS

Linestrider Tarot

Queen of Cups

KEYWORDS: *confidante, helper, introverted, intuitive, psychic, kind, sensitive, needy*

The queens have knowledge, experience, and authority and are concerned with individual or small group connections. The Queen of Cups is known for her sensitivity, kindness, and empathy, and she values relationships, peacefulness, and quiet introspection. While a good friend, she can be overly sensitive, needy, and even emotionally manipulative. Don't be fooled by her apparent absent-mindedness because she is more preceptive than she lets on.

SYMBOLISM 16: *Things That Are Held*

The Queen of Cups almost always holds an incredibly intricate chalice and gazes at it lovingly, showing her respect for and interest in relationships and matters of the soul. What people in the card hold can be a clue to what they value. What they are looking at can show their interest or main concern.

INSTANT ANSWER:
Reconnect with someone.

KING OF CUPS

Raven's Prophecy Tarot

King of Cups

KEYWORDS: *authority figure, power, experience, idealistic, empathetic, values strong ideals*

The kings have knowledge, experience, and authority and are concerned with large group and infrastructure/organizational situations. The King of Cups understands and controls his own feelings. These controlled emotions can sometimes burst out in unexpected ways. He has a kind heart, but good leadership, the greater good, and organization are his goals. Gain his support by balancing emotion with wisdom, experience, and a focus on the big picture.

TAROT TIP 21: *Court Card Ranks and Suits*

Each court card is associated with their suit's element. Pages are earth, knights are fire, queens are water, and kings are air. The Page of Wands is earth of fire, the Queen of Cups is water of water. The first element is their suit; the second is their rank. So, the King of Cups is air of water. In this image the feather represents air and the cup, water.

INSTANT ANSWER:
There are differences between controlling and repressing your feelings and between expressing and indulging them. Find the sweet spot.

Knight of Swords • Celtic Tarot

Swords

The suit of swords is associated with the element of air. While air is invisible, we see its effects. Air is a lot like thoughts, another swords connection. Worldviews, opinions about truth, communication; these are all part of the suit of swords. This suit traditionally gets a bad rap because many of the images are troubling. Our minds are powerful. They can be our greatest allies or our worst enemies. We don't always see it, but our thoughts affect our perceptions and even our reality. We can use our logic to untangle a knot, solve problems, or discern the truth. Conversely, we can create the biggest, hairiest knot ever or become obsessed. Add communicating with others whose minds are just as mighty as ours, and you can just imagine the potential chaos.

The swords court cards are associated with intelligence, wit, and rationality. They are precise and calculating, traits that can be a blessing or completely frustrating.

Because swords are connected to air, they are associated with the air signs in astrology: Gemini, Libra, and Aquarius.

Fairy Lights Tarot

Ace of Swords

KEYWORDS: *logic, intellect, reason, truth, victory, clarity, action plan, knowledge, communication*

The Ace of Swords is, like most swords, double-edged and therefore considered the most dangerous ace. The gifts of this card are clarity and truth. It really isn't the sword or its gifts that are dangerous; it is how you use this powerful weapon. Will you use it to cut through confusion and establish order or will you use it to wound someone? Words are our modern-day swords and can easily and deeply destroy others. The Ace of Swords is a precious gift. Wield it wisely.

SYMBOLISM 17: **The Ace of Swords**

> This sword is rising from the water, like Excalibur being offered by the Lady of the Lake. Combining air's authority and intellect with the intimate, healing power of water makes this particular Ace of Swords' focus about the great responsibility of great power. It doesn't so much tell what to do with the sword as much as it invites us to think about why we use it.

INSTANT ANSWER:
Speak your truth.

Mucha Tarot

Two of Swords

KEYWORDS: *reliance on logic, insufficient data, denial, feeling conflicted, distracting emotions*

Many cards in tarot encourage us to rely on our intuition, but here we are advised against that. She turns her back to the sea and the moon, symbols of intuition. Her blindfold indicates that the time of searching for more information is past. The decision will have to be made based on what you already know, your logic, and your ideals and values. This is not always a comfortable position, and you might be tempted to procrastinate, but those swords won't get any lighter.

SYMBOLISM 18: *Truce*

The Two of Swords almost always shows two crossed swords. In older traditions this represented a truce—not necessarily peace or reconciliation but a ceasefire. In this case we must stop fighting with ourselves and make an uncomfortable truce. We have to make a decision with probably insufficient data and also with the fact that our heart might prefer the other choice.

INSTANT ANSWER:
Do what you know to be right, even
if it is not what you want.

Three of Swords

Three of Swords

KEYWORDS: *unwelcome knowledge, painful truths, heartbreak, betrayal, disloyalty, unfaithfulness*

No one ever wants to see this card in a reading. It represents the all-too-common experience that often causes people to turn to a tarot reader. The image, no matter what deck, is clear: the heart has been pierced and is now broken and bleeding. It is tragic and makes us feel like our world has crumbled. Everyone says they want the truth, but the truth is sometimes really painful. Truth may come from the rational part of us, but we feel the pain in our hearts.

JOURNAL PROMPT 14: *When Truth Hurts*

In this card, someone knows a truth that will be unwelcome and has the need to tell you about it. Recall a time when you felt this in your life. How did you learn of the news that caused the heartbreak? Was there some way it could have been delivered to lessen the pain? Do words make truths harder or more painful? How do you share such truths with others to ease the pain?

INSTANT ANSWER:
Sharp words are like a slap in the face.

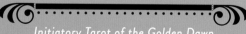

Initiatory Tarot of the Golden Dawn

Four of Swords

KEYWORDS: *rest, retreat, meditation, peace,
recovery, regroup, careful consideration*

The active energy of air finds rest in the number four.
This card often shows a warrior sleeping—a fighter finding peace, if only for a while. Here, the warrior is home
between battles, finding solace and refuge. Sometimes
the best way to get through a tough situation is to take a
break. Our culture isn't really into breaks but encourages
us to push through the pain no matter what. In the long
run, a short escape will actually make things go more
smoothly and quickly.

TAROT TIP 22: *When Cards Are Confusing*

If you have trouble interpreting a card or
understanding what it means in a reading, some
people will advise you to pull another card to
"clarify" the original. Resist that urge. Adding more
cards will just add confusion. Instead, leave the
reading out. Look at it once in a while, but don't
actively think about it. Let it roll around in your
subconscious. Allow the meaning to unfold.

INSTANT ANSWER:
Set aside your problem and come
back to it later with fresh eyes.

FIVE OF SWORDS

Vivid Journey Tarot

Five of Swords

KEYWORDS: *victory, defeat, humiliation, aggression, poor sportsmanship, success at a great cost*

The swords are about truth, which isn't always black and white. When two people compete, one wins, the other loses, so victory and defeat go hand in hand. In this card someone has clearly won all the swords. In the background is the defeated one, all but forgotten by the victor. This is a complicated card. Does it mean you win or lose? Did you win but make an enemy? Maybe it is asking you to simply rethink your goal since any outcome is going to be problematic.

TAROT TIP 23: *Description and Prescription*

There are different ways to look at a tarot card. You can combine them to provide the most useful readings. A descriptive approach describes what is happening (or will happen) in your life. The prescriptive approach prescribes actions to take and empowers you with advice so that you can take a more active role in crafting your future. Practice seeing both in each card.

INSTANT ANSWER:
You might win but the cost will be so high you'll wish you hadn't played. You know, like those carnival games where you end up paying $67 for a $3 prize.

6

Happy Tarot

Six of Swords

KEYWORDS: *journey, safety, escape, travel, assistance, impossible situation, protection, shelter*

Sometimes a situation can't be salvaged and leaving is the only option. The Six of Swords represents this hard truth. It suggests needing help from others to move from danger to a safe harbor. Relying on someone else may not be easy, especially if part of the problem was being deceived by someone else. Remember, just because one person hurt you doesn't mean that everyone will. Notice the swords in the boat. Getting out of the situation will not solve everything, but it will give you time and space to come to grips with the problems that still exist.

TAROT TIP 24: *Unequal Relationships*

The sixes in tarot show unequal relationships. Unequal doesn't mean bad or wrong. The Six of Swords shows someone helping someone else. In the cups it is an older person sharing kindness with a younger one. The pentacles shows a wealthy person sharing their bounty. The wands reminds us that heroes are in relationship with their community.

INSTANT ANSWER:
Do what you need to do.
If it's time to go, then just go.

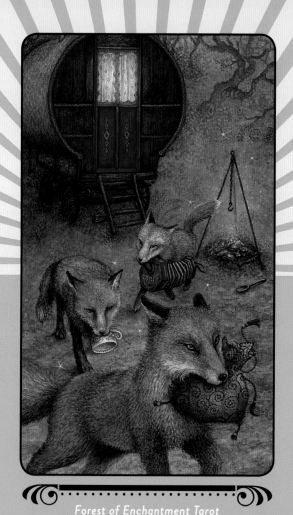

Forest of Enchantment Tarot

Seven of Swords

KEYWORDS: *stealing, rescuing, stealth, dishonesty, sabotage, sneakiness, traitor, spy*

This card is about someone taking something from someone else, but we don't know if it is a theft or a rescue or perhaps both. Foxes, known as sly tricksters, remove items from a camp without getting caught. Whether the plan is honorable or not, it looks like whoever is doing it will be successful. If this is you, consider a more forthright approach. If the situation is precarious, then be careful. Verify and protect first; trust second.

TAROT TIP 25: *Reading for Yourself*

Reading for yourself can be tricky because it is hard to be objective. It is really easy to spin the cards to say what we want. For example, most people see the Seven of Swords and assume someone is going to do them wrong. People hardly ever stop to question whether they are the one harming someone else.

INSTANT ANSWER:
Keep your friends close and
your enemies closer.

EIGHT OF SWORDS

Revelations Tarot

Eight of Swords

KEYWORDS: *feeling trapped, dangerous situation,*
limited options, helplessness, complex problems

Maybe you've figuratively painted yourself into a corner or were manipulated into a seemingly inescapable place. It would be easy to feel helpless, but escape is possible, although it might not be easy. Rely on cool intellect. Use the power of logic to cut the metaphoric ropes that bind you. It is easy to panic, but calm your emotions and quiet your thoughts. Eights are about speed, so find the first step that will loosen the knot and lead to a quicker than expected release.

TAROT TIP 26: *Reversals, Part 1*

There are lots of ways to read reversals. This image is from a very unusual deck that was designed to incorporate reversals. A deck like this gives visual tips about the reversed meaning. The swords involve communication. This image suggests that by using your voice—by speaking your truth—you can gain your freedom.

INSTANT ANSWER:
Use truth and reason to cut restrictions
before they get too tight.

Nine of Swords

Tarot in Wonderland

Nine of Swords

. . . .

KEYWORDS: *obsessive thoughts, sleeplessness,*
regret, worries, guilt, despair, oppression

Have you ever lain awake in the middle of the night with your thoughts racing? Our minds are powerful things, and thoughts can be as deadly as weapons. The Nine of Swords shows what happens when we turn these weapons on ourselves. For some reason, it is never the happy thoughts that visit us in the night. These nights come to us all, so it is smart to have a few techniques that can quell the racing thoughts so we can get the rest we need.

SYMBOLISM 19: *The Nine of Swords*

The swords here are shadowy illusions. They don't have heft unless we give it to them. The playing card emblems represent chance, while the chess pieces indicate the logic we can use to combat chaos. Nighttime thoughts might seem random, but if we look at the pattern they create, we can find clues to the theme that our subconscious is trying to show us.

INSTANT ANSWER:
It's always darkest before the dawn.
Things will look better in the morning.

TEN OF SWORDS

Ten of Swords

KEYWORDS: *surrender, ending, defeat, ruin, giving in, giving up, acknowledging an ending*

Not all battles can be won. No matter how hard we try nor how right we are, it is over and we can't change it. The tens also carry the seed of a new beginning. In the background the sun is rising. The advice here is to admit that you can't change this particular outcome, but you can get up, brush yourself off, and take what you've learned and try again. Or you can stay down and moan about the unfairness of it all. In that case, this becomes the card of the drama queen.

TAROT TIP 27: *Trimming a Deck*

Swords cut, so here is a tip about cutting. Tarot cards often have borders, and some people don't like them and cut them off. You can use a paper cutting tool, but I like to use scissors. Use a corner rounder (borrow or get inexpensively at a craft store). After trimming, gather the cards back into a deck and sand the edges with very fine sandpaper. This really makes the images pop.

INSTANT ANSWER:
The sooner you move on,
the quicker the pain will stop.

SKY KITTEN

Mystical Cats Tarot

Page of Swords

KEYWORDS: *message, supporter, enthusiasm, keen eye, gossip, lover of words, eager to begin*

Pages are young or inexperienced. The Page of Swords is super smart and loves to show off with an extensive and precisely used vocabulary. Give him a problem to solve and he'll surprise you with some creative out-of-the-box thinking. This page is prone to gossiping, meanness, and snobbery. If not laughed at and if his ideas are valued, he will be an amusing friend and valuable team player.

TAROT TIP 28: *Correspondences*

> Pages are always learning new things. If the Page of Swords studied tarot, he'd love all the charts of correspondences. There are tarot correspondences for lots of things: astrology, Hebrew letters, musical notes, colors, scents, crystals, herbs, and more. Pick something you love and see how it pairs with tarot.

INSTANT ANSWER:
How you say it is as important as what you say. Mind your words!

Shaman Tarot Deck

Knight of Swords

KEYWORDS: *focused, short attention span, serves truth and justice, dogmatic, relies on logic*

Knights are focused and have experience but lack authority. The Knight of Swords is motivated by ideas. His skills are language and communication. His weapons are logic, rationality, and evidence. He is fueled by the certainty that he is right. This makes him powerful and scary. He is brilliant, but if he isn't focused on a goal, he can create trouble. This knight is witty, but he gets bored easily if other people's stories are too predictable or mundane.

JOURNAL PROMPT 15: *Planning and Strategy*

What is your motivation or end goal in this situation? What would you like to accomplish? What are your strongest skills, and how can you use them to achieve that goal? What weapons or tools are available to you? What fuels you: proving yourself, helping others, creating something, keeping the peace, instigating change, promoting justice, or just trying to get through the day?

INSTANT ANSWER:
Before taking action, make sure you have a decent plan.

QUEEN OF KNIVES

Tarot of Vampyres

Queen of Swords

KEYWORDS: *ally, authority, quick-witted, clever, efficient, perceptive, cruel, hates deception*

The queens have knowledge, experience, and authority and are concerned with individual or small group connections. The Queen of Swords has been through tough times and learned hard lessons without becoming bitter. She cuts through confusion, makes plans, and discerns truth from lies as if by magic. Like a master chess player, she will help you help yourself while furthering her own aims. If you get on her bad side, you will likely feel the cut of her sharp tongue

SYMBOLISM 20: *Birds*

> Most images for the Queen of Swords show her with birds and butterflies, symbols of air. This queen comes from a vampire-themed tarot, so things have a slightly darker slant. A raven is ready to whisper secrets in her ear. Ravens bring to mind Odin's two companions, Thought and Memory. Maybe this is why she always knows what's going on and can discern truth from lies.

INSTANT ANSWER:
Stand up for yourself and do what you know is right, even if they call you really mean names.

King of Swords

Anna.K Tarot

King of Swords

KEYWORDS: *authority figure, decision-maker, intelligent, reasonable, controlling, clever, cruel, decisive*

The kings have knowledge, experience, and authority and are concerned with large group and infrastructure/organizational situations. The King of Swords lives by logic, evidence, and discipline. His goal is for everything to work efficiently while serving a clear ideal. He takes his responsibilities seriously and expects those around him to do so as well. If you want to engage his attention, be clear and to the point, avoiding emotional appeals.

SYMBOLISM 21: *The King of Swords and Chess*

> This image of the King of Swords is quite brilliant. Chess has a clear objective and rules. Every decision has consequences that can be deduced. However, when an opponent does something unexpected, the king has to think on his feet. He will probably enjoy the challenge as long as it doesn't happen often or upsets his preplanned and complex yet elegant strategy.

INSTANT ANSWER:
Stick to the facts and focus on the goal.

Six of Boons • Forest of Enchantment Tarot

Pentacles

The suit of pentacles is associated with the element of earth. Physical appetites, the need to create, and the desire for security are hallmarks of the pentacles. These cards are closely associated with our resources, such as money, time, health, and material items. From preparing a meal to building a grand cathedral, pentacles is the suit of making. The desire to live peaceful, safe lives can lead to laziness and greed. It is a short journey from stability to stagnation. This suit helps us to remember that wealth of any sort is meant to flow and that generosity more than avarice leads to an abundant existence. Acquiring things is only one part of the pentacles; stewardship is another. Caring for the physical needs of others, ourselves, and this planet that we call home is another more important aspect.

The pentacles court cards are often very concerned with the material world. They are usually good with money and making something beautiful out of practically nothing. Being naturally cautious, they may be considered boring by some, peaceful by others.

Because pentacles are connected to earth, they are associated with the earth signs in astrology: Taurus, Virgo, and Capricorn.

Ace of Pentacles

Green Witch Tarot

Ace of Pentacles

· · · · · · · · · ·

KEYWORDS: *abundance, resources, money, health, luck, achieving goals, small beginnings*

Arthur Edward Waite, the designer of the RWS Tarot, says the Ace of Pentacles is the "most favorable of all cards." This ace holds so much potential, and it's not just about money or worldly success. There is a spiritual dimension to this gift. Whatever gift this card represents may seem small and not very flashy. You might be tempted to write it off as insignificant, but this card advises against that. See beyond. See with creative vision. There is much more here than meets the eye.

SYMBOLISM 22: **Pentacles**

Pentacles in their proper orientation, pointing upward, signify the unification of all the elements under the guidance of Spirit. This is why the Ace of Pentacles is so powerful. When the pentacle is positioned to point downward (as often seen on the traditional Devil card), it means that the elements (including Spirit) are being used in service of worldly concerns.

INSTANT ANSWER:
Today is your lucky day!

TWO OF PENTACLES

World Spirit Tarot

Two of Pentacles

KEYWORDS: *multitasking, balance, tight budget, comparison shopping, calm in the face of crisis*

Do you ever feel like you are trying to do everything at once? If so, then you are living in the Two of Pentacles. Sometimes it is necessary, but it takes a lot of energy and should not be a permanent way of life. Try to face temporary chaos with calmness, knowing that you can do whatever needs doing until normalcy is restored. Maintaining this level of activity and anxiety for too long is devastating to our mental, spiritual, emotional, and physical health.

SYMBOLISM 23: *The Two of Pentacles*

The Two of Pentacles often has ships sailing on the rough seas, representing navigating challenges as you move toward your goal. In this image the lighthouse has a similar meaning: guidance toward a safe harbor. This can mean finding a calmer environment or dropping some of the balls you're trying to juggle, or both.

INSTANT ANSWER:
Is all that busyness really necessary?
Don't be a stress junkie.

Three of Pentacles

Steampunk Tarot

Three of Pentacles

KEYWORDS: *teamwork, creation, skilled work, worthwhile project, highlighting abilities*

Combine inspiration, excellent planning, and skill, and the result is usually phenomenal. The Three of Pentacles represents working as a team to achieve something that the individuals could not achieve alone or integrating all aspects of yourself to make something really special. If your current work doesn't inspire you, finding a deeper purpose will give life to your project. If a project isn't going well, make sure your intuition, reason, and skill are all playing a role.

SYMBOLISM 24: *How to Make Something Great*

> The arched doorway is part of a church, something that is in service to Spirit and the community. The man with the schematics is our logical side, planning so that everything works well together. The woman with the cards is our inspiration that gives vibrancy to a project. The woman on the bench is our practical skills and abilities that help manifest all that beauty in the real world.

INSTANT ANSWER:
Make something meaningful.

Four of Pentacles

Animal Totem Tarot

Four of Pentacles

possessiveness, managing resources, saving, protecting, stewardships, hoarding

Resources are tangible forms of energy, and energy is meant to flow. If it doesn't, it stagnates, like fruit left on the counter to rot. There are times when saving makes sense; we might need to save up for a large purchase or investment. It doesn't take much for common sense to turn to greed, hoarding, or paranoia. Learn to distinguish between when saving is really planting seeds for the future and when it is burying perfectly good food.

*TAROT TIP 29: **When to Save and When to Spend***

The Four of Pentacles can mean either scale back or let go. How do you know which? In a reading, look at the surrounding cards. If there are lots of cups, pentacles, or even-numbered cards, you are probably being too miserly. If there are plenty of wands, swords, or odd-numbered cards, there is a lot of chaos around your situation, so saving and being cautious is advised.

INSTANT ANSWER:
A penny saved is a penny earned.

5 OF PENTACLES

Mystic Dreamer Tarot

Five of Pentacles

KEYWORDS: poverty, hunger, bankruptcy, ruin, health concerns, rejecting help, isolation

We've all been here in some way, and it is never fun. The Five of Pentacles represents poverty of some kind: financial, material, or physical. Another kind of impoverishment is lack of community or network. This may be the most foundational poverty because if you have community, then you have a safety net. But community takes commitment and a willingness to help others when they need it. We value independence, so we often find ourselves alone.

JOURNAL PROMPT 16: *Community*

> What are your values surrounding physical, mental, emotional, and spiritual wellbeing? Is everyone responsible for themselves or are we our brothers' keepers? Is it hard to ask for help? Is it easy to give help without judgment or conditions? What kind of communities do you belong to, and how do they serve their members? What can people do on their own to create community?

INSTANT ANSWER:
Need something? Ask. Then turn around and help someone else before they ask.

Six of Pentacles

Tarot in Wonderland

Six of Pentacles

KEYWORDS: *charity, gift, loan, sound judgment, taxes, fees, sharing the wealth, asking for help*

The Six of Pentacles is about needing something that you have to ask or apply for, such as a grant or a loan. The resources are potentially available, but they won't just fall into your lap. You might have to jump through hoops and swallow your pride. Even then, sometimes there is an element of luck, especially if others are vying for the same resources. Depending on your situation, you may be the one holding the goodies and see that they are distributed fairly.

TAROT TIP 30: *Influencing Decision-Makers*

When approaching someone or an organization about funding, a king in your reading can give a clue about how to best prepare your case. Kings represent people with authority and means. The King of Wands suggests focusing on passion and action; cups, an emotional approach; swords, facts and logic; and pentacles, efficiency, effectiveness, and a good return on investment.

INSTANT ANSWER:
It is better to give than receive, mostly because it means you have enough to share.

7

PENTACLES

Seven of Pentacles

KEYWORDS: *assessment, evaluation, reflection, measuring return on investment, harvest, rewards*

You've planned, planted, and nurtured. Now, hoping for a successful culmination, you don't have a lot to do but wait for things to ripen. Use this time for assessment, considering what worked, what didn't, and what you can do next time to make things even better. Troubleshoot and make corrections. Have you done everything to support the achievement of your goal? This is applicable for projects but also applies to anything you're investing in, such as relationships.

TAROT TIP 31: **Tarot Journey Check-In**

How is your tarot journey going? Are you satisfied with how tarot is adding value to your life? Whether you are using tarot casually, occasionally drawing a card, doing a reading using a book, or committing to a deeper study of the cards, taking stock is a good idea. Identify your goals and make a sensible plan.

INSTANT ANSWER:
You will reap what you've sown.

8 OF PENTACLES

Thelema Tarot

Eight of Pentacles

KEYWORDS: *work, skill, craftsmanship, diligence, steady progress, satisfying work, attention to detail*

If you are like me, then you are always looking for short-cuts or that secret tip that will make whatever you are trying to master easy and almost instantaneous. The Eight of Pentacles is a sign that what you are attempting will need a lot of practice, learning from mistakes, developing muscle memory, and honing skills. This card has a dual energy. There is a quiet, almost meditative quality mixed with intense focus and determination.

TAROT TIP 32: *Positive Cards, Negative Positions*

When interpreting a positive card in a negative spread position (such as "challenge" or "what to avoid"), remember that all cards have a spectrum of meaning. For example, the Eight of Pentacles, when pushed to an extreme, can mean all work and no play, being stuck in a boring job, or being addicted to perfectionism.

INSTANT ANSWER:
If something is worth doing,
it is worth doing well.

9 OF PENTACLES

Silver Witchcraft Tarot

Nine of Pentacles

KEYWORDS: *discipline, individual achievement, material wealth, safety, security, solitude*

This card shows a rich and satisfying life crafted by your own determination, intelligence, creativity, and skills. This doesn't necessarily have to mean earning tons of money but rather feeling stable, productive, and fulfilled. You feel proud of your efforts. There is a little subtle advice in this card: note that she is alone. It's great to love your own company, but don't forget that good things are even better when shared.

SYMBOLISM 25: *The Nine of Pentacles*

This card usually includes a falcon. The falcon requires discipline to properly train. Falcons have keen intelligence, excellent vision, and intense focus. In this image the woman indicates silence. Quietly going about your work without broadcasting your every move also helps achieve your goals. Sometimes we talk about what we want to do more than we actually do it.

INSTANT ANSWER:
You are the captain and only crew of your ship, which means you not only set your course but also swab the decks.

TEN OF PENTACLES

Ten of Pentacles

KEYWORDS: *stable home, security, wealth,*
comfort, roots, plans for the future, connection

This card promises it all: financial security, domestic stability, and spiritual fulfillment. The Ace of Pentacles, the "most favorable of all cards," has fully bloomed and produced delicious fruit in the Ten of Pentacles: comfort, abundance, security, beauty. It can also represent things of value you enjoy that came from your roots. This could be a family business or inheritance. It can also be traditions and cultural practices or values that give your life meaning.

SYMBOLISM 26: *The Ten of Pentacles*

> The older person represents the gifts from ancestors; the child, the future; the young couple, the present moment; the dogs, domesticity and devotion. The banner shows the pattern of the Kabbalistic Tree of Life, indicating that their everyday lives are infused with and guided by Spirit. This is why the Ten of Pentacles is not just about money and worldly comfort.

INSTANT ANSWER:
Honor the past, celebrate the present,
and prepare for the future.

Page of Pentacles

Anna.K Tarot

Page of Pentacles

KEYWORDS: *message, supporter, prepared, mature beyond years, deliberate, doing things carefully*

Pages are young or inexperienced. The Page of Pentacles values hands-on learning, tangible results, and preparation. Don't mistake his quiet demeanor for stupidity. He is curious, loves experiments, and isn't afraid of what some might call failure. His easygoing nature makes him easy to be with. However, he can tend toward laziness or greed. Give him tasks and the freedom to experiment, and he will be happy and grateful.

SYMBOLISM 27: *The Page of Pentacles*

The pages are closely connected to the aces. This image of the Page of Pentacles shows both the nature of the page and of the ace. The Ace of Pentacles is potential that manifests in the real world and can be used to create even more abundance. Here the page uses his pentacle to acquire fish, showing a good investment of his resources.

INSTANT ANSWER:
Try something new without attachment to the outcome. You may just discover something amazing—or at least learn what not to do next time.

KNIGHT OF PENTACLES   CAVALIERE DI DENARI
CABALLO DE OROS   CHEVALIER DE DENIERS

RITTER DER MÜNZEN   MUNTEN RIDDER

Tarot of the 78 Doors

Knight of Pentacles

Knights are focused and have experience but lack authority. The Knight of Pentacles understands that it is not just what you have and how you use it but also when you use it. Timing is everything, and he is a master of knowing when to make a move for best effect. He is patient, resilient, and reliable. He may seem dull and may move slower than others (especially in our culture of busy busy busy). He is probably the most undervalued of the knights.

JOURNAL PROMPT 17: *Knights Good and Bad*

The knights are great journal partners because their strengths and challenges are really clear. Pull out the four knights and write about how you are like them, both their positive and negative features. How might the virtue of one balance the flaw of the other? For example, the Knight of Wands can be slowed by the Knight of Pentacles, calmed by the Knight of Cups, and directed by the Knight of Swords.

INSTANT ANSWER:
Timing is everything. Choose yours
wisely. Patience is a virtue.

Queen of Pentacles

Everyday Witch Tarot

Queen of Pentacles

KEYWORDS: *confidante, helper, accomplished, resourceful, generous, supportive*

The queens have knowledge, experience, and authority and are concerned with individual or small group connections. The Queen of Pentacles has excellent taste, solid values, and common sense. She is also magical because she can make any moment special with almost nothing. She loves natural settings. While her surroundings may be exquisite, she can be unobtrusive. She is not as showy, elegant, or witty as the other queens and can get stuck in ruts.

TAROT TIP 33: *Court Card Connections*

The court cards can be associated with other cards that can help expand your understanding of both. The kings show different aspects of the Emperor; the queens, the Empress; the knights, the Chariot; the pages, the aces of their suit. Try using the main qualities of the queens to write an interpretation for the Empress incorporating those traits.

INSTANT ANSWER:
There's no need to buy something new—mend or repurpose something, and it will do nicely.

KING OF PENTACLES

Tarot of the Hidden Realm

King of Pentacles

KEYWORDS: *authority figure, power, experience, creates wealth, values beauty, generous, practical*

The kings have knowledge, experience, and authority and are concerned with large group and infrastructure/organizational situations. The King of Pentacles has achieved many goals and created a comfortable life. Because he doesn't worry about his status or ego (although he will protect what is his), he is more generous and less demanding than the other kings. He knows that it is not just the stuff but the people to share it with that makes life worth living.

TAROT TIP 34: **Storing Tarot Decks**

Whether you see your deck as a spiritual item requiring respectful care or as a beautiful tool for creativity, you want to keep it safe. You can purchase or make a bag for your deck. You could purchase, embellish, or create your own box. A lovely scarf or length of fabric can both wrap your deck and be used for a cloth to do your readings on.

INSTANT ANSWER:
Be ridiculously generous.

Merlin/Hermit • Celtic Tarot

Chapter Five

READINGS

• • •

Doing readings is the most popular way to use tarot cards. Who doesn't have questions? Who wouldn't like a little guidance now and then? Whether you want to try your hand at predicting the future or discover new ways of approaching a tricky situation, doing a reading is the way to go.

Before trying a reading, the first thing you need to do is determine the type of reading. Not all readings are about telling the future. If you believe that the future is predetermined, then predicting the future makes sense; if not, then it doesn't. Instead, you can use the cards to better understand yourself, your situation, and possible courses of action.

Think about what you really want to know and why. How will you use the information? Consider the possible answers...ones you would love to get as well as those you wouldn't want to see. How will you feel if the answer is not what you hoped? A good rule of thumb is "don't ask if you don't want to know."

Speaking of questions, now is a good time to decide on your question. Don't worry about getting the wording perfect. Tarot is flexible, and unless you think the universe is like a lawyer looking for loopholes to trick you, any sincere search for guidance should give helpful results.

TAROT TIP 35: *Tiny Decks*

> Most tarot decks are a little larger than regular playing card size (around 3 x 5 inches). Some decks are also available in miniature (around 2 x 3.5 inches) as well as full size. These tiny decks are just so cute because the mini version of almost anything is just so cute. Small decks are practical, too, because they are easy to fit in a bag or pocket. Carry your cards anywhere, and always be prepared to do a reading on the go!

Once you have a clear idea about what you want to know, select a spread. If a spread doesn't suit your needs, you can alter it or even create your own. Designing spreads is another fun tarot activity, and if you are interested in how to do that, see my book *Tarot Spreads: Layouts & Techniques to Empower Your Readings*. For now, try the spreads included here. Most are general enough to apply to a variety of situations.

Pick up your cards and shuffle them however you like. Focus your mind and settle your emotions. Take a few long, slow breaths as you shuffle. You may like to say a prayer or state an intention, hold a crystal, light a candle, burn some incense, or play soothing music—whatever helps you to be in the moment and open to the wisdom of the cards is appropriate. Shuffle for as long as needed to reach a calm, receptive state.

TAROT TIP 36: *Fanning Powder*

Sometimes a new deck can feel stiff or even a little sticky depending on the coating used during printing. Shuffling is one of tarot's great pleasures. Make shuffling even better by coating your cards with fanning powder. Don't use talcum powder, which absorbs moisture and will make your cards even more sticky. Get real fanning powder from a magic or costume shop. It was created for stage magicians who do card tricks and is designed to eliminate friction. Fanning powder makes the cards move like silk in your hands. It is time-consuming to apply but so worth it. Put a generous amount of powder in a shallow bowl or plate with tall sides, large enough to lay a card flat. Coat the cards one at a time on both sides and rub the powder into the cards with a lint-free cloth. Wipe off the excess. After all the cards are coated, shuffle a few times on the cloth to remove any lingering powder.

· · ·

Now comes the moment of truth. Flip the top card over and put it in the first position of the layout, repeating as needed to fill all the spots. While leaving the cards face-down seems mysterious and flipping the cards over one by one can be exciting, it is easier to do a reading if you begin with all the cards faceup. A reading isn't just cards interpreted one by one with no relation to each other. A reading is the cards interacting together to create a whole that is more than the sum of its parts. Seeing all the cards at once gives you an instant sense of the situation.

TAROT TIP 37: *Reversals, Part 2*

> During the course of shuffling, your cards might get mixed up. Playing cards do not have a top-to-bottom orientation, but tarot cards do. When you lay your cards out, if any are upside down (where the top is at the bottom), simply flip them so they are right-side up. Upside down or reversed cards are used by lots of readers, but they are not necessary. Even some longtime professional readers do not use them. There is enough to discover in the cards, and reversals can complicate things. For now, don't worry about them. If you want, explore the idea after you are confident with the upright meanings.

• • •

Begin your reading by looking at all the cards without focusing on any individual card. Pay attention to interesting ways that the cards connect. Are certain figures in the cards looking at each other or away from each other? This gives an idea of communication between parties or of a lack of understanding. Because our eyes usually move left to right, we symbolically think of the left as the past and the right as the future. Are most or all of the figures looking to the left—and therefore stuck in the past—or to the right, focusing on the future? Does a symbol, shape, or color repeat throughout the spread? What does that suggest to you? Practice looking at the cards in a spread as a single picture and decipher what is going on.

• EXERCISE 3 •

What's the Story?

Without asking a question, without the intention of doing a reading, lay cards out in different spread positions or even a block of three columns and three rows (nine cards total). Imagine how an artist might use those images in that order to create a painting. Interpret the painting rather than the individual cards.

Individual elements or symbols will stand out, of course, but this approach brings a balance between the whole and the parts.

• • •

The suits have their own energy. If there is a majority of any one suit, then that energy is playing a role. The absence of a suit is important, too. Wands bring fast-moving, fiery, passionate action. Swords are also fast-moving but are more rational and in the mind rather than outward action. Cups are slower, with an emphasis on emotions, intimacy, and relationships. Pentacles are the slowest, bringing earthy, practical energy with a focus on material resources.

So a reading about a romantic relationship with a lot of wands but no cups can mean lots of attraction but no real intimacy or commitment. Because wands are fast energy, the relationship may burn itself out quickly. A reading about a job offer with many swords but no pentacles can mean a job with many challenges and a chance to really use your brain but limited financial compensation. Swords, being quick, can also indicate the ability to move up within the company.

Repeated numbers also add meaning to a reading. If you have two or more numbers in a reading, fold the meanings below into your interpretation.

Aces: beginnings, opportunities, gifts

Twos: decisions, choices, partnership

Threes: active energy, creativity, growth, teamwork

Fours: stability, structure, stagnation

Fives: conflict, loss, chaos

Sixes: communication, problem solving, unequal relationships

Sevens: reflection and assessment

Eights: power, speed, movement

Nines: completion, solitude

Tens: endings and resolution

• • •

Now start interpreting the cards one by one, adding detail and nuance to the overview you've created. To do this, blend the positional meaning with the card interpretation. Positions like past, present, and future (or possible outcome) are easy enough. Others require you to manipulate the meanings appropriately. For example, the Two of Pentacles in a position representing your strength in a situation could be the ability to juggle several tasks at a time. The same card in a position about a potential challenge might mean that you have too many things draining your attention and you are at risk for dropping one of the many balls you have in the air.

A lot of information can come up during a reading. Once you've interpreted all the cards, review everything you learned and organize it all into a coherent whole. If you are recording your readings in your journal, which I highly recommend, write out the final interpretation. If appropriate, create action steps based on the advice received. After the situation is resolved in real life, revisit your reading, making notes about what worked in terms of your interpretations. Also note places where the reading could have been improved based on hindsight. This helps you develop your relationship with the cards and your own personal meanings. Pay attention to card pairs or groups. Over time, you will notice if any of these repeat in other readings, further developing your interpretations.

TAROT TIP 38: *What Wasn't Asked*

Even though we try to think through our question and consider what information we need, we don't always know what we don't know. Our subconscious, our reason, and our intuition are all pretty good at reading between the lines and can often see what needs to be seen. To help make sure all the bases are covered, after interpreting a spread, look at the card on the bottom of the deck and read it as information that will be helpful but wasn't initially requested in the question. Because this card doesn't have a specific position, you have to trust yourself to interpret what it means and how it fits in with the overall reading.

• • •

Are you ready to try a reading for yourself? Here are a few spreads to get you started.

A Quick Reading

The quick reading uses only a single card and is fast, easy, and direct. There is no need to relate the card to other cards, no weeding through copious amounts of data. The quick reading is just a single card drawn in answer to a question. Even if you don't have a question, you can always pull a card and ask, "What do I need to know right now?" or "What card has something to teach me today?"

Three-Card Readings

While one-card readings are the quickest, three-card readings are among the most popular. They give you more cards to work with but not too many. You can use any of the following positional meanings for a three-card reading or come up with your own ideas. Use any three positions that make sense to you for your question. Once you decide what your positions are, shuffle your cards and lay them out in a horizontal row.

Past—Present—Future (or Possible Outcome)

The Dilemma—Choice 1—Choice 2

The Situation—Pro—Con

The Situation—Strength—Challenge

The Situation—Obstacle—Advice

Body—Mind—Spirit

Person 1—Person 2—The Relationship

The Situation—Do This—Don't Do This

• •

The Horseshoe Spread

This reading provides a clear snapshot of a situation, including the main challenge, the probable outcome, and advice.

1. *The past*

2. *The present*

3. *The future*

4. *You*

5. *The challenge*

6. *Advice*

7. *Possible outcome*

chapter five

204

The Celtic Cross Spread

This one is a staple for tarot readers and one that most people, even non-readers, are familiar with. It was invented by Arthur Waite, the designer of the Rider-Waite-Smith Tarot. Don't be afraid to modify any of the positions to suit your needs.

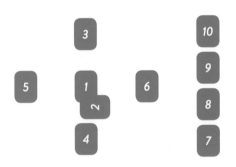

1. ***This covers you:*** what is affecting you or the situation

2. ***This crosses you:*** the obstacles or energies working against you

3. ***This crowns you:*** your ideal or goal in the situation

4. **This is your foundation:** the basis or root of the situation

5. **This is behind you:** influences that affected you or the situation but are now passing away

6. **This is before you:** what is likely to happen next

7. **Yourself:** how you see yourself in the situation

8. **Your house:** the influence of circumstances or people surrounding you

9. **Your hopes and fears:** your hopes or fears regarding this situation

10. **What will come:** the culmination, resolution, or outcome of the situation

• • •

These are just a few common spreads. You can easily find more in almost any tarot book as well as online. You can invent your own, too. Keep track of them in your journal so you can easily find one when you decide to use it. Practice with your favorites. The more you use them, the more comfortable you will get with them. Don't get in a rut, though. Even if you have a few reliable ones, try new ones to keep things fresh and interesting. You never know when you will find a new favorite.

JUSTICE

———◆———

Otherkin Tarot

Chapter Six

ACTIVITIES

• • •

Most people think about using tarot for readings, but there are other ways to use the cards. For example, you can choose a card of the day, journal with the cards, create affirmations, meditate to learn about the cards and get guidance, or create art based on the cards. If you want even more ways to play with your cards, see the further reading section for suggestions.

TAROT TIP 39: *Copying the Cards*

Because of copyright law, it is illegal to copy or use the cards for commercial purposes. However, when using the images for personal use, you can photocopy (or scan and print) the cards to glue in your journal. If you use a card for an affirmation, you can also copy the card to tape it somewhere you can see it or keep it in your wallet. Using photocopies means you don't ever have to pull a card out of your deck and potentially lose or damage it. If you don't have your own deck, you can use images from this book for the activities.

Card of the Day

One of the easiest ways to learn the cards is one day at a time. It is also a great way to practice applying the cards to your life. If you've already tried the bibliomancy exercise, you have an idea of how this works.

An advantage of the daily draw is that you can track your cards in your journal and pay attention to trends or themes that emerge over time. Does one card keep popping up? Are you getting lots of wands but never any pentacles? In this chapter you'll learn techniques that you can use to gain information from your long-term card of the day notes. It's like doing a long, slow reading over time.

When you are getting ready to start your day, think about what you are going to do. Is there anything that you would like advice on? Maybe you want some inspiration for the day. While shuffling your deck or before flipping through the pages of this book, think about what would be most helpful. Keep the question broad, like "What do I need to know about _____?" Or you can ask the tarot "What is your message for me today?" Another useful one is "What do I need to be aware of today?"

Once you have your question in mind, shuffle your cards and draw one. This is your card for the day. Without looking up the meaning, spend some time with the card. What story does the image tell you? Do any symbols stand out? If so, what do they mean to you? Do the numbers or names suggest anything to you? How does this card apply to your question? Write down your thoughts. Then, and only if you want to, read the card interpretation. How is it similar to your ideas? How is it different? What rings true for you? How, if at all, does the interpretation change your answer? Based on your answer, what action can you take?

At the end of the day, return to your journal and write about how the day went. How did your card of the day help you? Did what actually happened surprise you? Does this hindsight change your idea of what the card could mean? If this happens to you, don't feel like you "did it wrong," and don't let it discourage you. Even though there are many books about the cards, in the end how you interpret them will be a blend of traditional meanings and your own experiences, ideas, and intuition.

• EXERCISE 4 •

Card of the Day

At the beginning of your day, think about what you want to know for the day.

Pull a card.

Write out your ideas and how the card applies to your question.

Read the interpretation. Compare it to your ideas.

At the end of the day, review your notes, combining your ideas, the interpretation, and your experience that day into a personalized interpretation.

• • •

TAROT TIP 40: *Negative Cards*

Some people are afraid to get readings because they worry about getting negative cards. There are some cards in the deck that many people think of as negative based on the image or the name, such as Death, the Devil, and the Three of Swords. One of the reasons a tarot deck is useful is that it does show the whole range of human experience, which, as we know, includes the happy and the heartbreaking and everything in between. So, sure, there are cards that are more challenging than others. But these cards have the most to offer us, perhaps more than the overtly happy ones. If you get a card that feels negative to you, don't ignore it, and don't be scared. Challenging things happen to you all the time and you handle them and learn from them. Instead, sit with the card. What is it describing and what advice does it show? Remember that even the direst of cards has built-in solutions.

Journaling

Everyone knows about the benefits of journaling. Whether you already journal or not, tarot can either add to or even begin your journaling practice.

A dedicated journal is a great place to track your cards of the day. People who love bullet journaling might like to make a little graph for the front pages where you can track the cards and see at a glance which cards are popping up multiple times or what suits are absent from your life.

Here are some other ways to combine your journal and your cards:

Journal Prompt: You can pull a card and use it as a prompt and write whatever the card makes you think of, without concern for interpretation or trying to answer a question.

Freewriting: Pull a card and keep it facedown. Set your timer for five minutes. Flip the card and start writing without stopping until your timer goes off. Options: you can randomly draw a card, select a card you are interested in, or pick a card that you are having a hard time connecting with. Also, feel free to vary the time, using whatever works best for you.

Treasure Hunt: If you are having trouble figuring out a problem or processing an experience, go through your deck and find a card that reminds you of what you are thinking or feeling. Write about the card and why it reminds you of your situation. Then go on a treasure hunt in the image to find solutions or insights that may have eluded you.

• • •

Your tarot journal will become a place for creativity, learning, and, most importantly, to just enjoy your cards.

• EXERCISE 5 •

Tarot Journaling

Using your journal, your tarot deck (or the images in this book), and a pen (or your writing instrument of choice), try one of the three journaling activities: Journal Prompt, Freewriting, or Treasure Hunt.

Bonus: give all three a try and see what you like best.

• • •

TAROT TIP 41: *Selecting Your Tarot Journal*

Picking a journal is so personal. Use whatever you like best. Here are some things to consider based on my experience. A large journal with unlined pages will be useful when you start writing out your readings or doing art journaling. Larger pages will make it easier to glue in photocopies of the cards you are writing about. If you like using markers or fountain pens, find a journal with appropriate paper so your writing doesn't bleed through. I like either a spiral bound or lay-flat binding so I don't have to struggle to keep the pages open and can just focus on my journaling. My favorite, though, is to use a three-ring binder. This allows me to use any type of paper I want. Anything I can put in my three-hole punch works. Plus, I can move things around, making organization easy—especially if I change my mind about where I want something. Or, if I want something in two places, I can easily make a copy.

Affirmation

Affirmations help us become the people we want to be. An affirmation is a phrase written in present tense using first person. For example, "I am energetic and focused" or "I am kind and generous."

Combining an image with words makes an affirmation even stronger because it involves both your logical and intuitive sides. If your heart and mind are on the same page, it will be easier to create change in your life.

Think about what you'd like to affirm about yourself or what type of energy you want to express or draw into your life. Go through your deck (or the images in this book) and find one that best expresses that desire. Copy it and cut it out, leaving enough room at the top or bottom to write out your affirmation or desire. Put it up where you can see it regularly.

Another option is to let the cards guide you. Instead of consciously selecting a card, ask tarot to reveal an idea to affirm or attract. Shuffle your deck, randomly draw a card, and use it to create your affirmation.

• EXERCISE 6 •

Create an Affirmation

Pick a quality or trait that you'd like to develop in your-self or attract into your life.

Select a card that represents that idea for you.

Copy the image, cut it out, and write the statement at the bottom.

Place your affirmation where you can see it often.

• • •

Meditation

If you already meditate, you can use the cards to add variety to your practice. If you aren't into meditation, maybe using the cards will be just what you need to find your meditative groove.

First, decide how you will select the card you will use for your focus. If there is a card that you want to explore more deeply, go through your deck and find it. If you have a question or just want a message from the cards, shuffle your deck and randomly select a card while thinking about your intention, whether it is to find an answer to a specific question or to receive a special message.

Look at your card until you can visualize it with your eyes closed. Make yourself comfortable in a space where you won't be disturbed for at least five minutes. You can meditate longer if you want, but five minutes is a good starting time if you are new to meditating.

Take three long, slow, deep breaths. Starting with your feet and moving up your body, clench then relax your muscles and sink more deeply into your chair or whatever you are resting on. When you are ready, bring your card image to your mind's eye. Allow it to grow very large, filling your internal sight. Step into the image. Feel the environment, noting all the sensations you experience. Begin to interact with the characters or items in the scene. Maybe someone new will enter the area. Maybe someone will give you a gift or a message. Ask questions. Be courteous.

When you are done, thank anyone who helped you and exit the scene. Open your eyes. Move your hands and feet, slowly coming back into ordinary reality. Record your experience in your journal.

• EXERCISE 7 •
Meditation

Select or randomly draw a card and interact with it as you enter into the card through meditation.

Record what you learned in your journal.

• • •

Art Inspiration

Art is an important part of tarot. Creative expression is an important part of our lives. Many people do art journaling, keep a sketchbook, or dabble in crafts. Just like practically everything else, you can find ways to bring tarot into your creative endeavors. Here is a list of possibilities:

Copy a card: Use a deck you have, this book, or an internet search. Try to draw the card exactly as it is. This helps you focus on every element in the image and may lead to "I can't believe I didn't see that before!" moments. This is a fun way to get to know the cards, as you can think about what the card means as you examine it in such great detail.

Create your own version of a card: If there is a card you like or want to get to know better, using just your understanding of the card, draw, paint, or collage a version that expresses your ideas. You can use other cards for inspiration, but let this be your own vision.

Blend three cards into one: This is such a fun project and so useful, too. It helps you develop reading skills because you have to think about how the cards interact with each other to create a unique story. A common spread is just three cards representing the past, the present, and the future of a situation or question. A good reading is not just saying what the cards mean separately; a computer program can do that. A reader blends the cards together to create something altogether new. For now, don't worry about having a question or even thinking in terms of past, present, and future. Simply pick three cards at random and lay them out. Using elements from all of them or even just moods or feelings expressed in the cards, create a new piece of art (it can be any size, not just card-sized).

activities

Use photocopies of the cards to make greeting cards:
Pick the cards that go best with the sentiment you want to convey. For example, you can use the Sun for a birthday card, the Star card for a sympathy card, the Three of Cups for a girls' night out invitation, the Six of Cups for a thank you, and the Lovers, Two of Cups, or Four of Wands for a wedding card.

• EXERCISE 8 •

Make Art

Copy a card, make your own version, blend three into one, or make a card for someone. Or, if feeling wonderfully inspired, invent your own tarot art project.

• • •

Tarot cards are not just for readings. Maybe it is more accurate to say that readings can take many different forms. Using the cards can enhance almost any practice or activity. Using the cards in creative ways also helps you learn more about any particular card. Any of these activities can also be a way of finding guidance. As you bring tarot into your life, tarot comes alive.

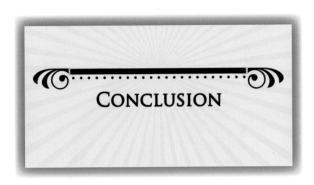

CONCLUSION

• • •

You made it to the end! You started out as the Fool, and now you are the World. Celebrate your newly acquired tarot knowledge and skills. Maybe mark the occasion by drawing a card or doing a longer reading about the next phase of your tarot journey. This is, after all, just the beginning. You can keep using this book for bibliomancy or to find activities to enjoy. If you are hungry for more, you are in luck. There are so many decks and books to explore. For more tarot book recommendations, see the further reading section.

May the cards be ever in your favor.

The World • Llewellyn's Classic Tarot

FURTHER READING

• • •

Sylvia Abraham, *How to Use Tarot Spreads*. Over three
   dozen tarot spreads.

Ruth Ann and Wald Amberstone, *The Secret Language
   of Tarot*. A study of common symbols used in the
   Rider-Waite-Smith Tarot.

Nancy Antenucci and Melanie Howard, *Psychic Tarot:
   Using Your Natural Psychic Abilities to Read the Cards*.
   Learn how to use your intuition to read the cards
   and how to strengthen your psychic abilities.

Melissa Cynova, *Kitchen Table Tarot: Pull Up a Chair,
   Shuffle the Cards, and Let's Talk Tarot*. A sassy, down-
   to-earth beginner-level tarot book.

Melissa Cynova, *Tarot Elements: Five Readings to Reset Your Life*. A set of five readings to push the reset button on your life.

Ethony Dawn, *Your Tarot Court: Read Any Deck With Confidence*. A modern approach to interpreting the court cards.

Ly de Angeles, *Tarot Theory and Practice: A Revolutionary Approach to How the Tarot Works.*. Includes basic card meanings and a very interesting method of conducting a reading.

Jaymi Elford, *Tarot Inspired Life: Use the Cards to Enhance Your Life*. If you want more ways, both meaningful and fun, to incorporate tarot into your life, this book's for you.

Josephine Ellershaw, *Easy Tarot Reading: The Process Revealed in Ten True Readings*. A fantastic explanation of how a reader weaves tarot card meanings into a seamless, useful interpretation.

Sasha Graham, *Llewellyn's Complete Book of the Rider-Waite-Smith Tarot: A Journey Through the History, Meaning, and Use of the World's Most Famous Deck*.

Poised to become *the* book on the influential RWS Tarot.

Sasha Graham, *Tarot Diva: Ignite Your Intuition, Glamourize Your Life, Unleash Your Fabulousity!* One of the best books ever for embodying the wisdom and wonder of tarot in your daily life.

Sasha Graham, *365 Tarot Spreads: Revealing the Magic in Each Day.* A tarot spread for every day of the year, plus the spreads can be used on different days for infinite flexibility.

Eden Gray, *Mastering the Tarot: Basic Lessons in an Ancient Mystic Art.* The book that influenced modern tarot and is still considered a good tarot primer.

Mary K. Greer, *Tarot for Your Self: A Workbook for Personal Transformation.* A tarot classic and the first and perhaps best guide to using the cards for personal transformation.

Mary K. Greer, *21 Ways to Read a Tarot Card.* An excellent book for deepening your understanding of tarot cards.

Kim Huggens, *Tarot 101: Mastering the Art of Reading the Cards*. A complete course in studying tarot cards to develop deeper meanings.

Marcus Katz and Tali Goodwin, *Around the Tarot in 78 Days: A Personal Journey Through the Cards*. A comprehensive course covering one card per day.

Barbara Moore, *Tarot for Beginners: A Practical Guide to Reading the Cards*. This book showcases how to read different decks by focusing on the images in relation to traditional Rider-Waite-Smith meanings.

Barbara Moore, *Tarot Spreads: Layouts & Techniques to Empower Your Readings*. A collection of spreads and instructions on how to get the most from them, the theory and practice of spread design, and lots of tips to make your readings more useful.

Sallie Nichols, *Jung and Tarot: An Archetypal Journey*. If you are interested in Jung and Jungian psychology, this book is delicious.

Robert Place, *The Tarot: History, Symbolism, and Divination*. A juicy, scholarly review of tarot's history.

Rachel Pollack, *78 Degrees of Wisdom: A Book of Tarot*. The book many of us cut our teeth on. A true tarot classic for a strong foundation.

Rachel Pollack, *Tarot Wisdom: Spiritual Teachings and Deeper Meanings*. A fascinating journey through the tarot based on Rachel's lifetime of studies, explorations, and musings.

Leeza Robertson, *Tarot Court Cards for Beginners: Bring Clarity to Your Readings*. An in-depth study of the court cards.

Leeza Robertson, *Tarot Reversals for Beginners: Five Approaches to Reading Upside-Down Cards*. A wonderful exploration of interpreting reversed cards.

Lisa Freinkel Tishman, *Mindful Tarot: Bring a Peace-Filled, Compassionate Practice to the 78 Cards*. A new approach to the cards to help bring peace and mindfulness to your questions and to your life.

Death • Marseille Cat Tarot

FEATURED DECKS

Animal Totem Tarot (Llewellyn: Leeza Robertson; art by Eugene Smith)   88, 170

Anna.K Tarot (Llewellyn: Anna.K)   46, 160, 184

Arcanum Tarot (Lo Scarabeo: Renata Lechner)   30

Book of Shadows (Lo Scarabeo)   50, 82, 114, 176

Celtic Tarot (Llewellyn: Kristoffer Hughes; art by Chris Down)   94, 132, 192

Everyday Witch Tarot (Llewellyn: Deborah Blake; art by Elisabeth Alba)   22, 84, 110, 188

Fairy Lights Tarot (Lo Scarabeo: art by Lucia Mattioli)   86, 134

Fairy Tale Tarot (Llewellyn: Lisa Hunt)   102

Fey Tarot (Lo Scarabeo: Riccardo Minetti; art by Mara Aghem)   52, 118

Forest of Enchantment Tarot (Llewellyn: Lunaea Weatherstone; art by Meraylah Allwood)   80, 146, 162, 236

Green Witch Tarot (Llewellyn: Ann Moura; art by Kiri Ostergaard Leonard)   164

Happy Tarot (Lo Scarabeo: Sevena Ficca)   122, 144

Hip Witch Tarot (Lo Scarabeo: Laura Tuan; art by Antonella Platano)   58

The Housewives Tarot (Paul Kepple and Jude Buffum, The Housewives Tarot, published by Quirk Books © 2004 by Headcase Design)   56

Initiatory Tarot of the Golden Dawn (Lo Scarabeo: Giordano Berti; art by Patrizio Evangelisti)   62, 140

The Linestrider Tarot (Llewellyn: Siolo Thompson)   128

Llewellyn's Classic Tarot (Llewellyn: Barbara Moore; art by Eugene Smith)   44, 224, 152, 182, 224

Lo Scarabeo Tarot (Lo Scarabeo: Mark McElroy; art by Anna Lazzarini)   54, 96

Magical Dogs Tarot (Llewellyn: Mickie and Daniel Mueller)   100

Manga Tarot (Lo Scarabeo: Riccardo Minetti; art by Anna Lazzarini)   38

featured decks

Marseille Cat Tarot (Lo Scarabeo: Lucia Mattioli)   40, 230

Mermaid Tarot (Llewellyn: Leeza Robertson; art by Julie Dillon)   112, 116

Modern Spellcaster's Tarot (Llewellyn: Melanie Marquis; art by Scott Murphy)   48

Mucha Tarot (Lo Scarabeo: Giulia F. Massaglia)   26, 136

Mystic Dreamer Tarot (Llewellyn: Barbara Moore; art by Heidi Darras)   78, 172

Mystic Faerie Tarot (Llewellyn: Barbara Moore; art by Linda Ravenscroft)   60, 92

Mystic Wizards Tarot (Llewellyn: Barbara Moore; art by Mieke Janssens)   90

Mystical Cats Tarot (Llewellyn: Lunaea Weatherstone; art by Mickie Mueller)   154

Mystical Manga Tarot (Llewellyn: Barbara Moore; art by Rann)   68

Next World Tarot (Cristy C. Road; Next World Tarot is under license, copyright 2017 Croadcore, the art of Cristy C. Road, all rights reserved)   64

Otherkin Tarot (Llewellyn: Siolo Thompson)   70, 124, 208

Pagan Cats (Lo Scarabeo)   76

Pagan Otherworlds Tarot (Linnea Gits/Uusi)   98

featured decks

Raven's Prophecy Tarot (Llewellyn: Maggie Stiefvater) 130

Revelations Tarot (Llewellyn: Zach Wong) 148

Rider-Waite Tarot (Illustrations from the Rider-Waite Tarot Deck® reproduced by permission of U.S. Games Systems, Inc., Stamford, CT 06902 USA. Copyright ©1971 by U.S. Games Systems, Inc. Further reproduction prohibited. The Rider-Waite Tarot Deck® is a registered trademark of U.S. Games Systems, Inc.) 28

Shadowscapes Tarot (Llewellyn: Stephanie Pui-Mun Law) 138

Shaman Tarot Deck (Lo Scarabeo: Massimiliano Filadoro; art by Sabrina Ariganello and Alessia Pastorello) 156

Silver Witchcraft Tarot (Lo Scarabeo: Barbara Moore; art by Franco Rivoli) 104, 180

Steampunk Tarot (Llewellyn: Barbara Moore; art by Aly Fell) 168

Tarot in Wonderland (Llewellyn: Barbara Moore; art by Eugene Smith) 66, 108, 150, 174

Tarot of Durer (Lo Scarabeo) 34

Tarot of the 78 Doors (Lo Scarabeo: Pietro Alligo; art by Antonella Platano) 186

Tarot of the Hidden Realm (Llewellyn: Julia Jeffrey) 32, 126, 190

Tarot of the Magical Forest (Lo Scarabeo: Hsu Chi Chun; art by Leo Tang) VI, 36

Tarot of the Sweet Twilight (Lo Scarabeo: Cristina Benintende) 42, 106

Tarot of Vampyres (Llewellyn: Ian Daniels) 158

Thelema Tarot (Lo Scarabeo) 178

Universal Tarot (Lo Scarabeo: Massimiliano Filadoro; art by Roberto De Angelis) 74

Vivid Journey Tarot (Llewellyn: Jessica Alaire) 120, 142

World Spirit Tarot (Lauren O'Leary) 166

The Wizard • Forest of Enchantment Tarot